COMPASSION AS A SUBVERSIVE ACTIVITY

—ıl‍ı.—

COWLEY PUBLICATIONS is a ministry of the brothers of the Society of Saint John the Evangelist, a monastic order in the Episcopal Church. Our mission is to provide books and resources for those seeking spiritual and theological formation. COWLEY PUBLICATIONS is committed to developing a new generation of writers and teachers who will encourage people to think and pray in new ways about spirituality, reconciliation, and the future.

COMPASSION AS A SUBVERSIVE ACTIVITY

Illness, Community, and the Gospel of Mark

David K. Urion, M.D.

Cowley Publications
CAMBRIDGE, MASSACHUSETTS

Published in the United States of America by Cowley Publications, a division of the Society of Saint John the Evangelist. No portion of this book may be reproduced, stored in or introduced into a retrieval system, or transmitted, in any form or by any means—including photocopying—without the prior written permission of Cowley Publications, except in the case of brief quotations embedded in critical articles and reviews.

Library of Congress Cataloging-in-Publication Data

Urion, David K.
   Compassion as a subversive activity : illness, community, and the gospel of Mark / David K. Urion.
      p.   cm.
   Includes bibliographical references.
   ISBN-10: 1-56101-279-3   ISBN-13: 978-1-56101-279-4
   (pbk. : alk. paper)
   1. Bible. N.T. Mark—Criticism, interpretation, etc. 2. Spiritual healing. 3. Miracles. 4. Reconciliation—Religious aspects—Christianity. 5. Community—Religious aspects—Christianity. I. Title.
BS2585.6.H4U75   2006
226.3'06—dc22
                                                                    2006017036

The names of the patients and families profiled in this book have been changed to protect their privacy.

Scripture quotations are taken from the New Revised Standard Version of the Bible, © 1989, by the Division of Christian Education of the National Council of the Churches of Christ in the United States of America. Used by permission.

Cover design: Rini Twait of Graphical Jazz, L.L.C.
Interior design: Wendy Holdman

This book was printed in the United States of America on acid-free paper.

Cowley Publications
4 Brattle Street
Cambridge, Massachusetts 02138
800-225-1534 • www.cowley.org

For Deborah, Kara, and Rufus

CONTENTS

ACKNOWLEDGMENTS

Books have many sources. The impetus behind this book was to offer a useful resource for the communities in which I live—families that deal with the consequences of serious illness in their children on a daily basis, the people who provide their care, and the communities that want to support them. In *Homage to Catalonia*, George Orwell noted that he could only write about one small theater in one campaign of a much larger struggle, but that he would endeavor to do so as truthfully and accurately as he could. Much, he noted, had been written from a great remove, and should be understood as such. I have been privileged beyond anything earned or deserved to have served as a physician to a group of children and their families at one particular institution over more than two decades. The stories and reflections I offer are therefore limited to that time, that place, and those situations, but I have tried to reflect upon them as truthfully and accurately as I could.

Books also require much support. I acknowledge with huge gratitude the support of the Reverends Mary Martha Thiel and Charles Kessler, my supervisors and instructors in Clinical Pastoral Education during a Kenneth Schwartz Fellowship at the Massachusetts General Hospital. The notion that telling our patients' stories could help us all understand our lives and work together first arose during that time. My fellow classmates—and the group of CPE alumni that still loyally meet once a month to reflect upon our lives and work—heard the early versions of several of these chapters, and I am grateful for their input and observations over the years. My spiritual director, the Reverend Curtis Almquist, SSJE, prodded me along when I was convinced this was a foolish enterprise, and put up with all manner of attempts to run away from this project. I cannot thank Michael Wilt of Cowley Publications enough for his patience and forbearance during this project. This manuscript was blessed by the editorial attentions of Ulrike Guthrie, who was everything one could seek in an editor—kind, gracious, honest, supportive, and possessing a keen ear for what I was trying to say. This book was made so much better by her deft editorial hand.

Several friends and colleagues read this manuscript in various stages, and offered thoughts and observations for which I am grateful: Will Slotnick and Karin Lindfors, the Reverends Mary Robinson and Mary Matha Thiel, Nancy Bassett, R.N., P.N.P., and Dr. Robert Truog. Thank you all.

I would not be a physician today if I had not met Dr. Pierre North when I was an exchange student at the University of Strasbourg during my undergraduate years. He is still my model of the ideal neurologist, one who practices with compassion, integrity, honesty, warmth, and humor. Meeting him changed the direction of my life and led me to this path. For all he offered, then and now, I am profoundly grateful.

My former department chair, Dr. Joseph Volpe, offered encouragement and support—moral, personal, and practical—that allowed me to pursue both CPE and the writing of this book. It has been an honor and a delight to have worked with such a wise and humane physician.

For years now I have been a member of a men's spiritual companionship group. These old friends—Drs. David Treadway and John Eckelman, Allen Rossiter, and Stephen Kennedy—have listened to early versions of these stories and have always responded in ways that help me to see more clearly.

Dr. David Shlim and Chokyi Nyima Rinpoche, Western physician and Tibetan lama, expanded my understanding of compassion by their remarkable teaching and example of the Buddhist tradition.

My family put up with my long hours of sequestering myself away in the attic and various other hidden spots while I wrote this; I am deeply grateful for their patience and loving support. My wife has always been able to ask difficult questions with grace and kindness, and I hope I listened carefully.

Most important, I want to thank the families and individuals who agreed to have their stories shared in this book. They have all reviewed their stories as presented here, and have all been satisfied that their privacy was sufficiently protected while the truths of their lives were adequately portrayed. I hope this book merits their trust and honesty.

INTRODUCTION

Radical Inclusion and our Baptismal Vows

—⫯⫯⫯—

Kyle's parents had come to my office, they said, for a second opinion about Kyle's condition. I knew the physician they had consulted before me, knew that he was careful, honest, and thorough. I knew that I would have little to add to his diagnosis, and also wagered that the parents knew this as well. So what was the real purpose of this visit? Did they hope, against all evidence, that there had been some mistake? Did they simply seek treatment from anyone other than the original doctor, the messenger who had dashed so many of their expectations, their high dreams and small hopes, for what the life of this child would be? Did they think I had some treatment for the untreatable, some cure that was not published in textbooks or medical literature, not spread across the Internet? Were they seeking some miracle? Why had they come?

I have tried, over the twenty years I have practiced pediatric neurology to learn to listen in these sorts of situations, to avoid the great temptation to fill silences with noise and sound, instead of waiting upon meaning and sense to emerge from the quiet. To allow the story to unfold at its own pace, to wait and see what happens. Patience is a virtue, without which no other virtue is possible; this is especially true in the practice of second opinions. In the clinical world I inhabit, the issue is rarely a matter of fact or diagnosis, particularly when the first opinion is from another academic medical center. Something else is playing itself out, and to rush in, to make assumptions about what that something else is, will only make it that much harder to find. A version of Heisenberg's Uncertainty Principle: the closer you try to touch something hidden, the more your seeking alters it. Defining the encounter, even in some benign way ("So, you were wondering if any other tests should be done in the context of your son's condition?" or "So, you wanted to see if we had any experimental treatment protocols that were not available at the hospital where you had been seen before?"), will invariably change it. The families I see, most of whom are polite and well-behaved, will follow my lead and engage along the path I have thus chosen. This may not be the path that led them here, and, if that is the case, some deeply felt question, some other yearning, will go unaddressed and unanswered. Often their true agenda is so hidden that even the family members themselves are not aware of it. Better to just listen, and watch what unfolds. Better to just ask, "How can I help you?"

So we talked, of Kyle's history, of his mother's pregnancy, the delivery, the newborn period. We spoke about his parents' extended families and what illnesses traveled through them. We talked of Kyle's development and his play, of his sleeping and eating, his elimination patterns and his daily rhythms. In the time we had, I tried to conjure up as complete an image as I could of this child's existence.

While his parents and I talked, Kyle himself sat in the corner of my office, rocking back and forth slowly, constantly making a small humming noise, lining up the toys strewn around him into a perfect row, just on the edge of a table. From time to time, he would look down the edge of the table, bringing one eye even with his row, making minute adjustments in the array, like a carpenter creating a piece of fine furniture. Two times with the right eye for every one time with the left.

After I examined Kyle, I sat down again and spoke with

his parents. I would have to agree with Dr. X, the first physician they saw, I told them. Their son had autism. All the
metabolic disorders that might prove treatable, and thus ame-
liorate his condition, had been sought by Dr. X. None were
found. Any possible confounding neurological diagnosis had
been considered, investigated, and eliminated as a possibility.
There was nothing else medicine could offer in terms of diagnosis or treatment. His progress would depend upon schooling
and therapies, effort, time, and patience. The family lived in a
town justifiably proud of its special education services, and the
school system had offered them a comprehensive set of therapies, involving practitioners in many disciplines: speech and
language therapy, early childhood education, physical and oc-
cupational therapy. It was a plan that would meet the highest
standards, the current state of the art in the treatment of autistic children. The family was one of means, and could supple-
ment these community resources with additional therapies.
There was nothing left to suggest in this quarter either.

And so, I asked, how are your own support systems? Raising
a child with autism is hard work, and often lonely. So many of
the conventional images of parenting in our society need to
be reimagined when autism is the context, the daily life that
is lived. The first soccer goal or ballet recital, birthday parties
and sitting in Santa's lap, first dates and first days of school—
none will occur in the same way that they do for most other
families.

Our extended families both live on the West Coast, Kyle's
parents said; they try to help, but distance and discomfort limit
what they can do. We have some friends, but most don't know
what to say or how to help. Nothing like this has happened to
any of them.

What keeps you going? I asked. What are your spiritual sup-
ports and beliefs that might help in a situation such as this? Oh,
they said, we are both Episcopalians. I nodded, as they started
to explain what that was, assuming that somehow I might not

have heard of this particular denomination. I said that I was an Episcopalian as well. Do you belong to a parish? I asked.

Yes, they said. When they became pregnant they decided it was time to go back to the religious community in which they had both been raised. Neither had attended church very often after confirmation, but the prospect of children brought them back. They visited several Episcopal parishes, and began attending one in the next town over from where they lived. It seemed family-oriented, they said, with a large Sunday school and an active children's ministry. There were many young families in the parish, but also enough older people, so that the couple's desire for surrogate local grandparents for their child might have a chance of being fulfilled.

The couple had been welcomed by a newcomer's committee shortly after they began attending services. They had met some nice people and made a few acquaintances. Not friends, really, they said, but people with whom they shared enough to feel comfortable. A group within the church had brought a few casseroles over after Kyle was born; the Baptism preparation class had been pleasant. The rector had been kind and attentive to the out-of-town relatives when they came for the Baptism.

During the first two years of Kyle's life, it gradually became clear to his parents that he was not developing along the lines their reading had led them to expect. They brought this up on several visits with their pediatrician, who at first dismissed their concerns with some observations about first-time parents and their worries. As their son's development more clearly verged away from the usual, however, their level of worry mounted. Finally, at an office visit for a fever and cough when Kyle was about twenty months old, they had insisted that something be done. He doesn't look at us, they said. He doesn't cuddle. He doesn't talk. Seeming rushed, the pediatrician finally arranged for the neurological consultation that eventually led to Kyle's diagnosis of autism. The couple recollected that the physician could not meet their gaze as he stated the diagnosis.

During this period of mounting worry and eventual medical evaluation, they had been bringing Kyle to the infant care provided at church. They were always told what a good baby he was, never causing any trouble, described as happily sitting in the corner, emptying all the toys out of a basket, putting them back in one at a time, and then repeating this process (always in the same order) until they returned to take him home.

When Kyle's parents were given his diagnosis, they were devastated. They admitted that they withdrew from many aspects of their lives, as they threw themselves into the therapies provided by the Early Intervention Program. Kyle's mother extended her leave of absence from her job, and stayed home to redouble the work all the therapists prescribed. Both parents withdrew from many people in their social circle—it was too painful to hear from other parents about the most recent achievements of their toddlers of similar age. One set of grandparents minimized the family's troubles, saying that "you and your brothers were all late talkers and look at you now— you never stop talking." The other set of grandparents would change the subject so quickly that it became clear that talking about Kyle's condition was off-limits.

The family stopped going to church. It was around Christmas, they said, and a sermon had been preached about God choosing to appear as a child. It painted such a rosy, sweet picture of childhood, Kyle's father said: images of innocence, delight, and wonder. The delight at the first steps. The wonder of Christmas through a child's eyes mirroring the delight God took in the world. The innocence of a child's smile. The sermon spoke of God made human experiencing all these things, things the couple had never experienced with Kyle, and felt they probably never would. "We just couldn't bear it," Kyle's father said in conclusion.

When the couple stopped attending church, the assistant rector left a few messages on their answering machine. Their absence had been noted. They didn't return the calls; they didn't know what to say. After a while, the calls stopped.

Months passed. When Kyle was three years old, he moved on to a special-needs preschool in the town's school system. He met a new set of therapists and teachers to whom he and his family had to adjust. It took time and energy. Kyle's personality was increasingly rigid; if he were to be thwarted in something, his usually placid disposition would turn on a dime. Suddenly, he would become enraged, throwing things and screaming, hitting himself and scratching his face. School personnel were infinitely patient, the family said, and taught the parents ways to cope with these outbursts. The family learned to avoid new situations that might bring on these symptoms, and coped as best they could when Kyle's explosions did occur.

One spring day, Kyle's parents decided to go back to church. They were not sure why, they said. Perhaps the ways the leaves looked, just coming out on the trees. Or perhaps the way the sun shone into their kitchen that morning. Or perhaps they were just too lonely to bear their lives without some form of community. The other parents in our son's special-needs class are nice, they said, but so driven. They are always on the Internet, or going to conferences, or seeing some new doctor they hear about. Their children have become their careers. The diagnosis of autism consumes them and their families. We just wanted to be a family, a little more normal, they said.

Their first foray into "normal" was going back to church. They arrived, and were greeted warmly by the assistant rector who had left messages for them. She swept them up, and brought them and their child to the preschool class. They were introduced to the teacher, a pleasant woman roughly their age, who had a child in this class. Kyle's parents tried to explain that their son was a bit . . . "different," the father finally said, but the teacher and assistant rector dismissed this claim with the affirmation that all children were welcome there.

Midway through the service, Kyle's parents became aware

of something happening in the back of the church. They saw the teacher pointing to them, and then one of the ushers came to the end of their pew. "Could you please come?" he whispered. "Something has happened."

Terrified, they left quickly, and ran down the hall and the flight of stairs to the classroom. They heard Kyle's screaming far down the hall. When they entered the classroom, Kyle was throwing books, blocks, crayons, anything he could grab, all over the room. The other children were in the opposite corner, with a teacher, all giving Kyle frightened looks.

The parents immediately began using the calming techniques they had been taught by therapists. After five minutes that seemed like forever, Kyle was calm enough to be taken out of the room. Parents and teachers all muttered apologies. Kyle's father noted ruefully that the adults' eye contact was as poor as their son's.

That afternoon, the assistant rector called. She wanted them to know that the other children were all fine, no one had been hurt. The parents were grateful for this, and said they had tried to explain that their son was different. He is autistic, they said. There was a long pause on the other end of the phone. I'm afraid we don't know much about autism, the assistant rector said. Another long pause. Well, the parents ventured, perhaps we should find some other option for our son—I don't think that class will work. Yes, the assistant rector said quickly, yes, perhaps that is best. You understand, we just don't have the training or the facilities. . . .

The family had never returned to church.

I sat and listened to this story in my office, trying to avoid my great temptation to sweep in with all sorts of practical, helpful instructions and recommendations. I thought that any advice or admonitions I could offer would have rung hollow, empty. In the face of their pain and loneliness, I thought that what they most needed at that moment was company. We sat, as the late afternoon sun began to reflect off the golden dome of the State House, and watched Kyle line up cars with great precision along the edge of my examining table.

I think there are neither heroes nor villains in Kyle's story, for it is not a classical narrative. I admire Kyle's parents for their steadfastness and devotion to their son, and to each other. Maintaining a marriage is not an easy thing in our society; doing so in the face of significant illness in a child is even more challenging. Teachers who work with disabled children show up every day and do extraordinary work that does not have the immediate rewards of the teaching I do, the manifest growth and development of already gifted minds and spirits. They do this work for wages below what they should receive and respect far below what this challenging work deserves. They are usually public servants, and unfortunately are often treated as such. Yet for all their goodness and hard work, these parents and teachers are not heroes in any classic sense. There is no flaw in their characters that has led to a tragic downfall. They have committed no acts of hubris, no challenge to the natural order. Kyle's life makes no sense as retribution or punishment for some misdeed. These are good people, greatly challenged and in some ways burdened by Kyle's disease, but they are not heroes.

By the same token, I don't think that the couple's extended family members can be seen as villains. Their reactions to Kyle show that they are afraid, limited, and unsure what to do in the face of a life as altered as one with autism is likely to be. Like most of us, when faced with a painful truth, they practice some form of denial or retreat. They so passionately wish it not to be so that they cannot accept its reality. They are in good company.

In the central story of our salvation history, those closest to Jesus refuse to understand where the road to Jerusalem leads until they see him taken away as a common criminal; they hide or deny him after the arrest. It is a moment, a place, that we all inhabit throughout our lives, when the true nature of a significant loss or pain in someone we love comes crashing down on us. The grandparents and relatives of this boy are human in their desire to avoid a painful truth, but they are not villains. In their responses to Kyle, there was no intentional infliction of pain, no embracing of large or small evils. Likewise, the church personnel in Kyle's story display flaws, but are not villains. The assistant rector and Sunday school teacher were so caught up in their vision of community that they simply failed to listen. The family, haltingly, had tried to tell them something about their son, and they had not been able to hear the story behind the words. They are in good company, too. In the gospel, we are all admonished to listen: Let those who have ears hear. Usually, most of us fail to listen. Our failure is a serious human flaw, but it does not make us villains.

There are, however, saints and sinners in this story. Sinners, in the sense that anything we do that separates us from the love of God, the extraordinary graciousness of God, is sin. And we have been told time and time again that everyone, everywhere and at all times, is included in the embrace of a loving God. That enigmatic kingdom of God, which we are promised is very near to us, does not exclude on the basis of any human category. All of us—the sick and the well, the mentally gifted and the mentally challenged, the gentle and the angry, the strong and the weak—we are all included in this embrace. Anything we do that fails to recognize in the face of anyone we encounter today the face of a brother or a sister is sin. Just as surely as my exasperation with a family that doesn't give their child her anti-seizure medications for the ninth time and again ends up in our hospital's emergency room is an occasion of sin, so was the fear, discomfort, or misplaced identification that led the assistant rector and Sunday school teacher in Kyle's story to accept the family's offer to disappear. Anything that divides the community that God has declared to be one is sin.

And there are saints: Kyle's family, his teachers, the assistant rector, the grandparents, the Sunday school teacher—everyone in this story, at some place in their heart, longed to do something good for Kyle. We all fail every day, but the very desire to try again defines our nature as that transcendent category Paul uses to describe us all—saints. We have embarked upon a journey that brings us ever closer toward God, and no matter how circuitous our route, how halting our steps at times, no matter how much we need others to carry us for parts of that road, we are always and everywhere returning to our one true home. Our recognition that this life is a journey from exile toward home is the act that makes us saints, for that recognition has embedded in it the knowledge of God's overwhelming love and care for each of us.

When Kyle was baptized, the congregation present stood in for all the rest of us, the entirety of humanity, what we call the body of Christ, and promised that we would do all in our power to support Kyle in his life in God. It is a promise of terrifying proportions to make for anyone, for any child, but all the more so for a child with a neurological disorder as afflicting as Kyle's. How do we support him in his life in God? How do we even understand the life in God of a child who does not speak or interact with other people in any way we can fathom? How can we embrace a life so deeply hidden?

As a community, we have not kept our vows with children such as Kyle. We have broken faith with his parents. Our community is thus diminished by this rupture. We are in need of healing, as much as Kyle and his family are. What God has never seen as anything but one people, one community, we have put asunder.

In this book I want to consider the lives of children and families who live with major neurological disorders. How can we understand these illnesses in the context of our faith in a loving God? How could a loving God allow such lives to be? How do we understand healing in this context? If so much is made of miraculous cures in the central story of our faith, what are we to think of lives that have not experienced such miracles? In the scriptures, dead children are brought to life, people possessed by demons are restored, hemorrhages are stopped, lepers are made clean—but not all dead children, not all demoniacs, not all who bleed, not all lepers. How do we understand those who do not receive miraculous healing, in the context of our faith in a loving God? How do we incorporate them and their families into our community?

How do we build the new Jerusalem so that none are excluded? We are told that the kingdom of God is very near and that among its attributes is a radical inclusiveness. How do we approach that kingdom, bring it into our midst as communities of faith, particularly in light of children and families as different from ours as the one I have described?

I want to consider the lives of children with major neurological disorders through the lens of our life as a community of faith. Our tradition focuses on the Incarnation of Emmanu-el, God with us. We also believe that we are for each other the presence of the living God, the body of Christ in this broken world. Each of us may be all we see or know of God today. If this is so, then how do we understand the life of a chronically ill child as another form of this incarnation? How do we see the face of Christ in the face of a child like Kyle, a child with autism?

My chief identity is as a baptized person who was led to become a physician to children with developmental disorders. I am defined by these two conditions on a daily basis. Just as a magnet is defined by its two poles, which draw some things near and push others away, these two conditions create the tension and energy in my life. The vows made for me at Baptism, later embraced as my own, create one set of conditions by which I have chosen to live. I have accepted the sevenfold gifts of the Spirit, and have promised that I would do everything in my power to support every other member of the community in their life in God.

My identity as a physician has created another set of

conditions by which I have chosen to live. The process of being incorporated into the world of the physician has been so consuming, so complete for me, that I cannot remember what it was like to think in any other way. I choose the word *incorporation* quite intentionally, because its roots are so similar to those of the spiritual concept of *incarnation*. I live and move and have my being as a physician, just as I live and move and have my being as a baptized person. These dual aspects of my identity create a set of conditions that define how I desire to approach life. This incarnation of mine evolves in the overlapping, enmeshed communities of faith and medicine in which I live.

I will use the Gospel of Mark as the chief textual lens through which to consider the lives of children with neurological disorders. I choose Mark because it is the earliest of the gospels, and thus most closely reflects the sense of community that the early followers of the Jesus movement espoused. I also choose Mark because it is the version of the gospel story that was told by and for a community that was marginalized— not rich, not near the levers of power, not smiled upon by fortune—Galileans, hill people, poor people. The lives of children with neurological disorders are also marginalized, their concerns usually far removed from the central issues of our life as a society. Mark is a good traveling companion on this journey.

Although the name of the medical unit I direct includes the term *disability*, I do not like the word. In the early days of my stewardship of this unit, I tried to change its name. The change was unsuccessful because it caused great confusion in the referring community: Where, the referring physicians wondered, had the services we provided for the disabled gone? Still, I am uncomfortable with the term, not because it is politically incorrect, but because I do not think it conveys what we mean with any accuracy. *Disabled* comes from the Latin root *habilis*, which means "to be skilled or adept." We thus define two categories of people: those skilled at being human—the able-bodied—and those whose skill is lacking or deformed in some way—the disabled. This dichotomous notion of humanity is one I have come to reject.

I prefer to describe children like Kyle as having a neurological *disorder*. Their lives are not *ordered* as creation would have them be. This description suggests that the deepest issue concerning such children is not one of identity (the sort of person one is, able or disabled), but rather a disruption in the relationship between these children and the community. It suggests that the issue is as much the community's as the child's. Persons are disordered to the extent that they are not incorporated into the community. The moment they are incorporated into the community is the moment they cease to have a disorder; the medical condition they have may, or may not, persist, but their disorder ceases because a small part of creation has been restored.

Similarly, while we have come to call the episodes of healing described in the gospels as *miracles*, this word reflects a later attempt to understand the events described. The term used in Mark for these healing moments is *deeds of power*. The chief actors in most of these stories are Jesus and his disciples Peter (the Rock) and James and John (the Sons of Thunder). The imagery conveys action, power, and force. These are not images that conjure up rosy sunsets or beams of soft light, with angelic choirs softly humming in the background, but events that shock and jar us. Words such as *terrified, amazed*, and *awe* usually appear in the text after one of these events. These are events that shake the complacent disorder of the community and wrench it back toward the intended order.

I want to contemplate the "miraculous" healings described in the Gospel of Mark from this vantage point: as subversive political acts of power that provide examples of restoring the integrity and the wholeness of the community, not just for the persons who are overtly healed but for the community as well. The kingdom of God that is at hand, that is very near to us, is just this: the poor, the sick, the outcast. Their integration into the community heals them and the community, and restores creation to the radical inclusiveness with which it began. These tales of power we will consider reflect upon the extraordinary and paradoxical power of the powerless. In these stories, God takes weak and fallible human form to restore creation in its totality—to include the weak, the lame, the blind, the deaf, and all of the afflicted as equal members.

After I had heard the story of Kyle, I sat with his parents in the gathering dusk in my office. Finally, I again asked Kyle's parents the question with which I had started: How can I help you? After a long pause, Kyle's father, in a small voice that choked back some tears, said, "Be with us. Keep us company. This is so lonely."

This book is part of my attempt to keep that promise, a promise which we all made to this family on the day of Kyle's Baptism. We vowed to do everything in our power to support them in their life in God. We said we would do all we could to bring the kingdom of God near by participating in the king-dom of God. That kingdom is based upon a radical inclusive-ness that heals us all.

1

The Power of the Powerless
to Restore Community

—ılı.

MIRACLES

—Ⅲ—

Adam's parents came into my office with their six-year-old son, pulling him in a small red children's wagon cushioned with pillows and a blanket. Adam was extraordinarily floppy, and his eyes roved around the room as a result of a retinal degeneration I knew I would see upon examination.

I remarked to Adam's parents that, according to their records, Adam hadn't been seen by a neurologist for several years now. A child this ill would usually be under the rather close watch of a neurologist, and would have significant involvement with a number of agencies providing care in the home. Adam probably needed frequent turning and physical therapy for his chest—given the sound of his breathing and his obvious secretions—and suctioning as well. He probably needed such attention every few hours, and such care would be exhausting for the family alone, without some outside help and specialized equipment.

Adam was also fairly big for his age, and I thought that it must be difficult to get him from bed to bath to cart and back again, without someone's back or arms giving out. Adam's family would have needed what insurance companies call "durable medical equipment" for some time.

I wondered if the parents' lack of follow-up might mean they were somehow neglecting Adam's needs, which would be cause not only for alarm but also for reporting to governmental authorities. As a so-called mandated reporter, I would be obligated to report them to the Department of Social Services if I so much as suspected neglect, or risk losing my medical license. And yet Adam appeared well-nourished, well-cared for, obviously loved.

Perhaps, I thought, Adam's parents had rejected traditional Western medicine, and sought alternative treatments. This is common, in my experience, among families with children whose diagnosis has no known conventional medical cure or treatment. Watching a child slowly die of an incurable disease is one of the most painful things a parent can experience; to do nothing but provide comfort measures in response to this slow death is intolerable for some families. They need to struggle actively against the disease. If Western medicine has no treatment options, then they seek alternative approaches.

All of these thoughts raced through my mind as Adam's parents sat looking at their boy, stroking his hair and cleaning his face.

Yes, they said, they had seen Dr. Q in our department several years ago, when Adam began to lose ground. He had developed normally until he was about three years old; then he had begun to slow down. Eventually, he stopped walking. He began to "forget things," ultimately he stopped speaking. He lost his vision. Before they consulted with Dr. Q, they had seen several other doctors, who had all been puzzled. Dr. Q, however, had told them at the first visit what disease she thought Adam had.

It all made sense, what she said, the mother observed. Everything we had observed could be explained by Dr. Q's diagnosis, and several things we hadn't told her she sort of predicted, or said were very likely. She said she had to do a blood test to confirm the diagnosis, and we should come back in about six weeks.

They came back, and the diagnosis was confirmed: a form of degeneration of the myelin, the essential insulating covering around parts of the brain, spinal cord, and nerves. As the insulation falls apart, the electrical messages being sent get scrambled. Arms and legs no longer respond to commands from the brain; thinking and memory become clouded, speech garbled. The result is the gradual dissolution of voluntary control of the body, as well as the distortion and decline of the mind.

We could do a biopsy, Dr. Q had said, but I doubt it would provide any new conclusions. She told Adam's parents that the disease was hereditary, *autosomal recessive*, meaning that each of them carried half of the "bad gene." (They remembered that quite clearly—"There was something bad about our coming together as a couple, to produce this in our boy," they explained.) Any future pregnancies would have a one out of four chance of the same thing happening.

The disease is progressive and fatal, Dr. Q told them. There is no treatment. She told them that Adam had probably less than six months to live. They should go home and make him comfortable, she said.

Dr. Q escorted them to the elevator, they remembered. She dropped off some of their insurance paperwork at a secretary's desk on the way there. Do they need a follow-up appointment, Dr. Q?, they remembered the secretary asking. No, she had said, no follow-up will be needed.

At this point in their story, the parents paused, and we all watched Adam, lying there on his bed. As they had spoken, he had turned his head slightly toward their voices. He smiled.

So, the father said, we went home. Time passed—four months, six months, eight months, a year, two years, more. He's still alive. We thought maybe we should come back. You know, not that we think the diagnosis is wrong—we've read a lot about the disease since Adam was first diagnosed. He has all the signs and symptoms they write about in children with this disease. It's just that he seems to be sort of stable now, and maybe we should be doing something differently. I mean, I don't know. Adam's still alive. It's not really a miracle. I mean, just look at him. How could this be a miracle? But he's still alive. We were wondering what we should do. Now.

Miracles are a difficult and thorny business for us in today's world. Whatever the nature of our work or livelihoods might be, we have all been raised and educated in a society that takes certain ideas as so central to our understanding of the universe that we do not even recognize their presence in our thinking. We believe in a certain universal order, what are often referred to as the laws of nature. These rules or governing principles have been elucidated, we all know, by scientists and investigators over several centuries. While we may know very little about the process by which these "laws" were "discovered," the general image in our popular culture is one of a heroic figure—the scientist—struggling against forces of superstition, cant, or dogma to uncover some tidy truth or precept that was actually present in the universe since its beginning.

In the West, this process is often viewed as being at odds with organized religion, especially the Roman Catholic Church. If asked about the rise of the scientific worldview, many people might recall a story such as Galileo's, in which a lone figure is seen valiantly championing the Copernican model of the solar system against the massed forces of the Inquisition, a caricature of organized religious oppression. They might also remember that Galileo was forced to recant his views under threat of death or torture, and did so. His alleged remark, under his breath, "Yet still it turns" might also be recalled.

That this sketch does not conform to many of the facts of the matter shows the power of the mythology of Scientific Progress. That Galileo was a far more complex human being than this plaster hero portrayal, that his process of work was far more nuanced and infinitely less straightforward than imagined in this myth, and that the conflicts between Galileo and the members of the Roman (not Spanish) Inquisition were far more complicated than this story admits, are all quite true, but perhaps slightly beside the point for the purposes of our consideration of miracles. The myth is recounted because it reinforces what has become a dominant worldview in the West, a view we might call Scientific Triumphalism. Science, imagined in this view as some unitary process quite independent of the culture and society in which it arises, is seen as a force that continually moves in one direction—from Ignorance and Superstition toward some Absolute Truth.

The images of scientists in popular culture usually portray a lone person, laboring away in obscurity to prove some point of which he or she is certain: Newton wrestles with understanding the forces that bind the universe together, and sitting under a tree "discovers" gravity. Fleming sits in a laboratory, puzzled about why there are circles free of bacteria on the Petri dishes contaminated by mold, and "discovers" penicillin. Pasteur struggles in his laboratory, finding that small organisms, not Evil Humors or Bad Air, cause disease. Jenner suggests that inoculating people with a less virulent illness such as cowpox will protect them from the dreadful illness smallpox. The rest of the world rejects these findings as nonsensical and laughs at the Hero who proposes them. The Hero perseveres, mounts evidence and data, and then, suddenly, The Truth dawns on the world and something hidden is now revealed. Newton's theory explains and predicts the movement of heavenly objects. Penicillin saves countless lives. Small boys are cured of rabies, and milk is made safe. Smallpox is eradicated. We move ever forward, from Error into Truth, through the lone, heroic struggle of wise and brave scientists.

None of the working scientists I have met recognize their work in these popular portrayals; rather, they think of what they do as complex, often contradictory, and fundamentally an activity of inventing models that might explain some part of the universe's myriad functions, rather than uncovering immutable "laws" of nature. They do not view their work as particularly heroic, usually do not work in isolation, and are frequently quite unsuccessful in any given task or experiment. Science is a messy process, full of blind alleys, wrong assumptions, and false starts; and at times it can become a rigid dogma of its own. Yet our society has as one of its central myths the concept of Progress. And Progress, in the sense of an advancing of a particular form of highly individualistic, commercially driven, money-based evolution of society, needs a set of central stories or beliefs, just as any mythology does. Science, portrayed as an ultimately unstoppable, majestic progression from Error into Truth, Darkness into Light, serves as the unifying myth behind this view of Progress, so common in the West since the end of the Renaissance and the beginning of what we call the modern era.

The Enlightenment, particularly in its English and Scottish forms, saw the rise of a view of the universe as an enormous clockworks: infinitely complex, delicate, even arcane, but susceptible to analysis and reason. This view of the universe suggested that all events had a proximate cause that could be figured out by appropriate study and investigation. And once the operations of these causes were deduced, the process in question might be harnessed for commerce, industry, or improved scientific agriculture. Unlike the late Renaissance, during which the concept of Natural Philosophy arose in opposition to Roman Catholic doctrine, the mythology of Enlightenment Science did not so much compete with Christianity as it did co-opt it. Protestant Christianity, with its implicit—and sometimes explicit—rejection of the mystical and the ecstatic, its emphasis on individual piety at the expense of collective obligations and organic communal relations, was well suited to be interpreted in a light that favored rationalism, progress, and empiricism.

To see how these ideas were expressed, just look at the verses of a hymn familiar to many of us: "The Spacious Firmament on High," whose words, by Joseph Addison (1672–1719), are a paraphrase of Psalm 19.

The spacious firmament on high,
With all the blue ethereal sky,
And spangled heavens, a shining frame,
Their great Original proclaim.
Th' unwearied Sun from day to day
Does his Creator's power display;
And publishes to every land,
The work of an Almighty hand.

Soon as the evening shades prevail,
The Moon takes up the wondrous tale;
And nightly to the listening Earth
Repeats the story of her birth;
Whilst all the stars that round her burn,
And all the planets in their turn,
Confirm the tidings as they roll,
And spread the truth from pole to pole.

What though in solemn silence all
Move round the dark terrestrial ball?
What though nor real voice nor sound
Amidst their radiant orbs be found?
In Reason's ear they all rejoice,
And utter forth a glorious voice;
For ever singing as they shine,
'The Hand that made us is divine.'

Notice the differences in tone and emphasis between the hymn's version of Psalm 19 and the recent translation of the psalm that appears in the New Revised Standard Version:

The heavens are telling the glory of God;
and the firmament proclaims his handiwork.
Day to day pours forth speech,
and night to night declares knowledge.

There is no speech, nor are there words;
their voice is not heard;
yet their voice goes out through all the earth,
and their words to the end of the world.

In the heavens he has set a tent for the sun,
which comes out like a bridegroom from his wedding
    canopy,
and like a strong man runs its course with joy.
Its rising is from the end of the heavens,
and its circuit to the end of them;
and nothing is hid from its heat.

The law of the Lord is perfect, reviving the soul;
the decrees of the Lord are sure,
making wise the simple;
the precepts of the Lord are right, rejoicing the heart;
the commandment of the Lord is clear,
enlightening the eyes;
the fear of the Lord is pure,
enduring forever;
the ordinances of the Lord are true
and righteous altogether.
More to be desired are they than gold,
even much fine gold;
sweeter also than honey,
and the drippings of the honeycomb.

Moreover by them is your servant warned;
in keeping them there is great reward.
But who can detect their errors?
Clear me from hidden faults.
Keep back your servant also from the insolent;
do not let them have dominion over me.
Then I shall be blameless, and innocent of great
    transgression.

Let the words of my mouth and the meditation of my
  heart
be acceptable to you,
O Lord, my rock and my redeemer.

The images of the created universe and the place of humanity within that universe are quite different in these two versions of Psalm 19. The universe of the psalmist, as it appears in the NRSV, places humanity within a created order, as part of a vast but wonderfully intimate universe. While day and night are recognized as inherently silent, they are the sources of speech and knowledge. The images of the sun are domestic—a bridegroom adorned to meet his bride, an image often to describe the relationship between God and God's people, and one that Jesus uses throughout his ministry. The images are dynamic—for example, that of a strong man running for the sheer joy of it. The image of the athlete in *Chariots of Fire* comes to mind: "When I run, I feel His Pleasure."

Yet for all this wonder at the sheer unbridled marvel of creation, the purpose of this contemplation of the universe in the NRSV translation is clear: to order human relationships and to keep them rooted and directed by the will of the Lord. Wisdom, that particular combination of knowledge and right action, will be provided even to the simple, we are told, if we keep to the ordinances of the Lord. Sensations, experiences, and pride-filled human counsel may deceive and misdirect us, but a constant yearning for the ways of the Lord will protect us from this waywardness. The nature of the universe is one of constant desire to be aligned with the ways of the Lord, and to be within this eternal order—to be parts of its flow—brings harmony, righteousness, and redemption. To be within this created order puts one in right relationship with the Creator and all of creation.

Psalm 19 has a dramatic arc, beginning with the image of the day bringing us speech and the night bringing knowledge, and ending with a prayer, the prayer we often hear before a sermon: a prayer that words of our mouth, our speech, our days as the psalmist calls them, and the meditations of our heart, our knowledge, our nights, may be always acceptable in the sight of the Lord. In other words, the totality of our lives, the sum total of our days and our nights, recapitulates the universe itself, contains the universe itself, with its days and nights, our speech and knowledge, both grounded in the ordinances of the Lord. A life hidden in God is a life in right relationship to God, the universe, and the rest of humanity. It is a life rich and sweet, both treasure and nourishment.

In contrast, Addison's "The Spacious Firmament on High," although based on Psalm 19, looks at the universe from a much different vantage point. In the hymn, the place of humanity in the glorious structure of the universe is limited to that of an awestruck observer, rather than that of an intimate participant. The hymn confines itself to considering the heavens, far removed from humanity, the world, and all its messiness. The metaphors in Psalm 19 that connect humanity to the heavens and the psalm's inclusion of the breadth of humanity—the wise and the foolish, the proud and the humble, the honest and the deceitful—are nowhere to be found in Addison's hymn. The domesticity and physicality of Psalm 19's images are replaced by details emphasizing the vastness of the heavens and the arrangements of its parts: exquisite, but remote. In "The Spacious Firmament on High," the rules of the universe are confined to the regulation of the orbits of the planets, the placement of the stars in the heavens, the alternation between night and day. There is no association made between the celestial realm and human activity, no representation of day and night as speech and knowledge, intimate human events. The cosmic system Addison describes is removed from human activity—magnificent, awe-inspiring, but having little to do with the day-to-day conduct of human life. We look up at the heavens, but our gaze is not then drawn back down to regard one another in a transformed or redeemed way. The hand that made this universe is divine, but it appears that this divine hand is not involved in human life. In Addison's version of Psalm 19, we can sit, and wonder at the majesty of the created universe, but this majesty does not inform our daily actions or our choices. All of these concerns are absent from the hymn.

This view of the universe as being set in motion by the Creator, who is then absent from its subsequent workings, was characteristic of the Enlightenment. This Deist view, so common among intellectuals during the birth of modern experimental science, still permeates the popular conception of science. We can have either biology or religion, reason or wonder, it argues, but not both.

In this view, miracles can be approached with a sort of calculus and proved to be an explainable part of everyday experience. John Littlewood, a British scientist who died in 1977, actually proposed a Law of Miracles. He defined a miracle as an event of apparent special significance to the observer which occurred with a probability of less than or equal to one in a million. Based on this definition, he calculated that everyone experiences a miracle once a month. Events, he argued, occur roughly once per second, that is, the brain processes sensory experiences at roughly this rate. We are awake and able to experience such events between eight and ten hours per day. If we do the appropriate calculation, we experience between 864,000 and 1,080,000 events per month. One of these events is likely to occur only once over a given period and be interpreted by the observer as having some special significance for him or her. Hence, Littlewood argued, it would be interpreted by the observer as a miracle, and thus everyone experiences a miracle once per month. This reductionist thinking also explains the apparent frequency of miracles in certain lives, he argued. Nothing out of the everyday is actually happening; certain people are simply more aware of their environment and therefore more primed to note the infrequent event that is defined as a miracle.

For persons of a rationalist bent, this explanation of miracles allows one to keep Scripture as a sort of guideline for moral behavior, while interpreting the so-called supernatural events described in the Bible through a different lens. This construct suggests that the rabbi Jesus was a wise, ethical teacher who offered comfort to many. When some persons who followed Jesus experienced a spontaneous remission of their illness, as will happen in all illnesses, his devoted followers interpreted this infrequent event with special significance because of their love for Jesus, and called it a miracle. Calculating the length of his ministry and the frequency of such events, it is not surprising, say these rationalists, that we have a handful of such stories recounted.

Of course, the rationalist interpretation does not address an important question: Why would this itinerant teacher of wise aphorisms, whose followers attributed explicable if infrequent biological events as miracles wrought by his hand, be perceived as such a threat to the Roman Empire that he would be sentenced to crucifixion, a death reserved for political opponents and rebels against the Empire? The rationalist view also fails to account for healing as a political act and compassion as a subversive act, because it separates the miraculous event from its community context. It disrupts the ecology of the deed.

We can consider the limitations of the rationalist perspective by examining the origin of the word *miracle*, which derives most directly from the Latin root *mirare*, meaning "to admire" or "to wonder." Miracles, then, can be thought of as actions on the part of the Almighty that cause us to wonder, to admire, to stand in awe before the Presence. It is the nature of that miraculous encounter that differs in the two versions of Psalm 19 that we have been considering. In Addison's hymn, we stand in a meadow during the summer and look up. The vastness of space, the planets in their orbits, the moon in its progression across the month, the sun in its seemingly never-changing rising and setting—as we contemplate this entire intricate dance, we are filled with awe. Yet this limitless cosmos, so delicately regulated and intertwined, is described as far removed from us. It is not connected with our daily lives, our struggles, our desires, our hopes. In Addison's version of Psalm 19, we may be worshipful spectators, but our lives are not engaged, nor our conduct clearly influenced, by our contemplation of the heavens. The emotional tone of "The Spacious Firmament on High" is one of distanced admiration and gratification that this universe is not random in its organization, but the question of how to order our own lives does not enter into this contemplation. The hymn describes one sort of miracle—a sensation of awe and wonder at the ordering of the universe. Yet this miracle is in the end a cold one—remote and removed from our daily existence, our small joys and private woes. It is a miracle that delights our rational minds, but ignores the struggles and contradictions of our hearts.

In contrast, the version of Psalm 19 that appears in the NRSV attempts to connect us—our lives and experiences—with our contemplation of the created universe. In this consideration of the created order, the rules of the Almighty are described with certain attributes that bind the universe together. The law of the Lord is called "perfect," in that it not only orders the heavens but revives the human soul. It is called "sure," not just because the planets stay in their courses but because it makes simple people wise; that is, allows them to combine knowledge with right action. The law of the Lord is called "right," not just because of the serene and precise beauty of the heavens but because it warms and rejoices human hearts. It is called "clear," not just because of the certainty with which the motions of the heavens are established but because human eyes can be enlightened by it. It is called "pure," not because of the remote and austere beauty of the night sky but because its place in human hearts endures forever. Finally, the law of the Lord is called "true," not just for what we can see by examining the heavens, but because it establishes righteousness in human conduct.

In the NRSV version, Psalm 19 is deeply entwined with daily human existence, which the psalmist acknowledges can be difficult—full of faults, often dominated by people of impure intent, full of those who demean others, full of trickery. In this version, our contemplation of the heavens, the marvel of creation, is only worthwhile to the extent that we see in the universe the reflection of the divine order in our own eyes. Such contemplation is not meant to elevate us from the mundane, but rather to help us live it better, to make us wiser, clearer, kinder, more alive, and more rejoicing.

Addison's version of Psalm 19 is a poem deeply steeped in admiration and wonder at the miracle of creation. This is the effect that one understanding of miracles can have. We stand back in awe and wonder at the healings that are described throughout the Gospel of Mark. I think, however, that these miracles, or deeds of power, are actually rooted in another understanding, another kind of piety, which is reflected in the NRSV version of Psalm 19. These deeds of power not only restore the kingdom of God, but also include and invite us in. We are asked to be participants in these healings and restorations, in that we are asked to reestablish right relationships in our hearts with the rest of the community. We are asked to re-found the kingdom of God as imagined by the psalmist, and live it out through the healing ministry. We are asked to join in full participation with all of the created order—the sick, the lame, the blind, the oppressed—to accept them as equal members of that kingdom. We are asked to go beyond a passive admiration to an active communion with all of creation. Mighty deeds of power are thus not limited to particular acts of Jesus, but include our acceptance of his invitation to be a full participant in the kingdom of God—by embracing the lame, the blind, and the oppressed as full members of our community, which is the entirety of creation, without exception or exclusion.

The deepest root of the word *miracle* is the Sanskrit word *smytate*, which means "he smiles." These mighty deeds of power are not acts at which God desires us to tremble in fear, to quake or cover our faces. They are mighty acts of healing of the community, of the re-establishment of right relationships between various parts of the created order. Those who were excluded are now brought back in. The severed parts are quite literally *re-membered*. The lost are returned. And in the midst of this profound reconciliation, this gathering together, He smiles.

So Adam, the boy in the red wagon, had experienced a mighty deed of power, a miracle in the oldest sense. He had an illness, an incurable one, but his family had loved him and included him in a very profound way within their family. They spoke of him with warmth and tenderness, and not in the "third-person invisible" I so often hear us use in hospitals, the tendency to talk of a sick or injured child in the room with us as if that child could not hear or understand what we are saying. Adam's parents spoke of him with love and light in their voices, and Adam turned toward that love, just as we turn our face toward the sun after a storm passes by. Adam turned toward that part of the eternal love which his family, incarnated, and he smiled.

Adam's family now sought to enlarge that circle. They offered me, and by extension the rest of my department, a place within their community. That, too, was a mighty deed of power: to be given a place within their closest circle was a deep and profound blessing. In the midst of my helplessness before the steady and relentless progression of Adam's illness, my inability to offer any treatment that might slow or reverse the course of his disease, I was nonetheless offered a place within his community. To acknowledge that we had all done everything in our power for Adam, and we could do no more—and still be welcomed as part of his community—was a great gift. Adam's parents accepted him, despite his limitations, as a full and perfect member of their family, and they accepted me, with my limitations, in the same way. It was an act of profound generosity.

Some months later, I bumped into some fellow parishioners, a married couple who had a second home in the same community where Adam's family lived. My friends had spent much of their summer in the community, and had attended the local parish. Talking over coffee, the husband said, "You know I never really heard the words of baptism before last week." I expressed my surprise, since they had raised their children in the parish, one of whom was now a member, as was their grandson. They had attended any of a number of baptisms of their own brood, and the husband and I had served together as Lay Eucharistic Ministers for many more. "No," my friend explained, "I mean I never thought about what we really promise for children in baptism. You see, last week we went to this remarkable baptism. The child was obviously impaired in some way—the kind of child you must see in your work every day. He's a big boy, the family pulls him in a wagon. I guess a wheelchair wouldn't work. He's just so floppy. Anyway, when we got to the part where we promise, out loud, to do all we can to support this child in his life in Christ, I asked myself, 'Do I really mean that? I mean, here and now. This child?' And I thought, yes, I guess so. But how hard that is going to be! I mean, for any child that is quite something. But for this child, we've got our work cut out for us. "

We are all asked to do everything in our power, whatever that is, to support the baptized in their life in Christ. For a child like Adam, the very act of visibility, of still being here and part of our community, is a mighty act. It speaks of perfection and certainty, righteousness and clarity, purity and truth. In his identity and totality, Adam is accepted just as he is into the community. Not as flawed member in need of correction, but as a full member whose identity is accepted. His illness does not define him, but just as surely it is part of him. By acknowledging Adam, we take one step toward embracing all of creation with lovingkindness and compassion. We take one step toward that elusive kingdom of God which is just outside of our vision.

Like something we see best with our peripheral vision at dusk, the kingdom of God is best seen not by looking at it directly, but by looking into the face of a child like Adam and seeing nothing but the face of God. He smiles.

COMPASSION AS A
SUBVERSIVE ACTIVITY

—Ⅲ—

Rebecca had been brought to the Intensive Care Unit at the hospital where I work. A baby girl, whose arms and legs were spread out and flaccid, with intravenous lines entering her at the crease of one elbow and into the groin—signs that someone had wanted to deliver a large amount of fluid and medicine quickly. A breathing tube entered her mouth, taped in place so that much of her small face was obscured. Rebecca was not breathing on her own; the ventilator was doing the work for her. Monitors hummed and beeped; two nurses were getting her settled in after transport from another hospital.

"Near-miss SIDS," the house officer said matter-of-factly, using the acronym for sudden infant death syndrome.

"Didn't miss death by much," added the senior resident, the young woman at his side.

"The numbers don't look good—a lot of end-organ damage. Wanna take a look at her for us, Doctor Urion? Family's not here yet, but we'd like to get an idea of how bad it is overall before we sit down with them." She looked too tired and too sad for as early in the day as it was. "The story we have is a bit sketchy. Family put her to bed last night, after feeding. Uneventful day, not sick, no sick contacts. Didn't wake up for her usual 2 A.M. feeding; mom got up at 3 A.M. and realized the baby hadn't awakened them. Found her cold and pulseless in her crib."

"Crib?" asked the fellow, who had joined us at the bedside.

"Yup. Crib. Not co-sleeping, according to the story we have from the transport team. Didn't roll over on her."

"Well, I guess that's a mercy, somehow," said the fellow.

The house officer looked puzzled. The senior resident, picking up on this, added, "Some studies suggest that a lot of SIDS is actually suffocation from infants sleeping with adults. The parents get exhausted, and roll over on the infant in their sleep. At least in this case that won't add to the parents' guilt."

"If it's true," added the fellow.

The nurses said they were set, and I examined Rebecca. There was no evidence of any higher brain function on examination, and the reflex responses the brainstem generates were tenuous at best. The brainstem, that part of the brain that controls automatic functions such as breathing, heartbeat, and sleep/wake cycles, had been injured fairly severely; the upper part of the brain, the cortex, seemed even worse off. These conditions all argued for profound deprivation of blood and oxygen for a significant period of time. They were likely to be associated with very significant permanent brain injury if the infant survived at all.

"Nothing much on board to explain this," said one of the nurses, meaning that sedating medications which could mimic brain injury had not been given, and that she acknowledged the results of my examination without my saying anything directly. "They gave some rock at the outside ED for the intubation— God knows why. She couldn't have been moving much," by which she meant that someone at the other hospital had given Rebecca a paralyzing agent (rocuronium) often used to make the placement of a breathing tube for artificial ventilation easier in a struggling, sick child. Its use in Rebecca was curious, perhaps a reflexive response of the staff in the other emergency department. Rebecca would metabolize the medication more slowly now because of the organ damage she had experienced, but the nurse was correct: Rebecca's coma was not caused by medication.

I arranged for the tests that we needed to determine how extensive Rebecca's brain injury was: a CT scan to evaluate the brain's structure, and an EEG to look at the brain's function. They were both consistent with a very severe injury to the brain, probably because of a long period deprived of blood and oxygen. There were findings on both tests that suggested a high likelihood of significant problems if Rebecca survived. Infants with test results like these are often left blind, unable to move independently, unable to feed themselves, unable to interact with their families.

Rebecca's parents arrived, driving in from a fairly long distance to our hospital. They sat with their little girl, the father stroking Rebecca's hair, the mother standing beside the bed and looking numb. Rebecca's father kept whispering her name, over and over again; the mother began to sniffle, then sob, then let out a huge, keening wail. Father led her away, her head buried in his shoulder. They went to a small private room, just off the main waiting area for the intensive care unit.

The senior resident paged me when Rebecca's parents were ready to sit down and talk with us. We sat in a circle, in a room all of us except the parents had sat in before, with other bereft families. We had all delivered the news that all parents fear, sitting in this little room. If the phrase "time of trial" from the Lord's Prayer means anything to me, it is times like these—when your child is sick beyond all recovering. Your child has a tumor, and the surgeons cannot operate. Your child has been injured beyond our ability to help. Your child has an infection we cannot treat. This little room is firmly planted in the valley of the shadow of death.

The senior resident was calm, frank, gentle, and weary. She introduced herself, as did the rest of us—Rebecca's primary nurse, the fellow, the unit social worker, me. The parents' surname was an old one in New England; one of the original white settlers of the island where my family has some land carried that name. This family was from a town up the coast, a fishing port that had fallen on hard times. Rebecca's father was a mechanic, her mother had once worked in a big box store, but stayed at home after Rebecca was born. This was their first child. Father had many tattoos, a shaved head, and a short beard. Mother stared at her shoes throughout the entire conversation.

"Your baby had a period of time when blood and oxygen weren't being supplied to her organs, because her heart and lungs stopped working. We don't know why this happened; we're in the process of investigating that. Her liver, kidneys, and heart have all been hurt by this period of time without blood and oxygen, but usually this degree of injury does not lead them to shut down permanently. We won't know for sure for another day or so, but the blood tests suggest that those organs will recover." The senior resident took the lead in this conversation. The fellow stood by, able to step in if she stumbled. This is the way of teaching hospitals; there is ultimately no way to learn to do something, even deliver bad news, without actually doing it. The senior resident had sat in on many of these conversations over her years of training; she was now viewed as being sufficiently grounded that she could lead the discussion.

"You said, those organs will recover," said the father.

"I should have said, probably will recover," said the resident.

"Whatever. What you didn't say anything about was the brain. What about the brain?"

"That's why we asked Dr. Urion to come. He's the neurologist, the brain doctor."

"I know what a neurologist is," the mother said through clenched teeth, staring at the senior resident with burning eyes. "We're poor, not stupid." Father put his hand over hers, and stroked it. She began to sob.

He looked at me, and said, "So, what about the brain?"

I looked at them both, and said the information we had was from several different sources: Rebecca's physical examination, her brain wave test, the X-ray pictures of the brain—tests of structure and of function—they all pointed in the same direction. Rebecca's brain had been very badly injured, and so far was showing no signs of recovery. It was too early to tell if she was going to recover brain function. We would need to wait and watch.

"So how long? How long before we know?"

I said I thought that the next two days would probably give us an indication of which direction the brain was heading: toward some recovery, or not.

"There's nothing we can do except wait, is there? I mean, no medicines or anything that would help the brain get better?"

I said that beyond supporting Rebecca's other body functions, and keeping a close watch for any signs of swelling of the brain, there wasn't anything else specific we could do.

"Brain swelling?"

I said that after such injury, the brain often became swollen with water, a result of the shutdown, sometimes death, of cells. The injured brain cells take on water, which in turn makes it more difficult for blood to get to the uninjured cells. The pressure inside the skull increases as a result of this swelling, pushing back against the heart, which is trying to pump blood into the brain.

"I'm a mechanic for boat engines," Rebecca's father said. "I know about taking on water."

We sat in silence for a while. After a few minutes, the senior resident asked if the parents had any other questions.

Rebecca's mother, not looking up from her shoes, said, "I just don't want her to live like a vegetable."

A day passed, and Rebecca's other organs began to show signs of recovery. Her brain did not.

Walking around the unit, making rounds on the patients we were seeing there in consultation, I came by Rebecca's bedside.

"Got a minute?" Rebecca's father asked.

"Sure."

"Let's just step outside, okay?"

He kissed his wife on her forehead, kissed his daughter on hers, and then we stepped out to the waiting area and sat down.

"You got children? I mean, probably none of my business, but I need to know. I mean, we're gonna be talking about some hard stuff, and I need to know if you have children. If you know what it's like, even a little."

Yes, I had children.

"Daughters? Sons?"

One of each.

"And I can see from the ring you're married."

Yes, that's true.

"Best things I got in this world are back in there. Only reason I'm here is them. I mean that. I was a hell-raiser, pure and simple. 'Spose you can tell by lookin'," he said as he flexed his arms and showed his tattoos, smiling ruefully.

"I met my wife in a store," he continued. "I was pickin' up some stuff. She worked there. Something about her just grabbed me. Like the whole place just blew away, and there she was. Know what I mean? She was just something. I found an excuse to go there every day for two weeks, before I screwed up the courage to ask her out.

"She said, 'I know all about you, and I'm not like that. I don't run around with the kind of boys who run around with the kind of girls you do.' She had me dead to rights.

"I asked if she thought people could change. 'Maybe,' she said.

"Anyway, I did change, is the point, and I convinced her. I gave up drinkin' and smokin' and hell-raisin'. I worked hard. Made foreman at the shop. We got married, and got a place of our own.

"Then, she got real sad. I mean, like they said she was depressed. Had to go into the hospital for a while. 'You should just leave me, forget me, find someone who isn't so bad off,' she said. But she'd stuck by me, and I stood by her. She got better, sort of. I mean, she took medicine, and met with a therapist, and she got back to getting dressed and cleaning up and smiling sometimes. They said it was, like, hereditary or something. Her mom was that way, and an aunt. I guess that was supposed to make me feel better. It didn't.

"Then we got pregnant. God, that was great. She was just so happy. They warned me, her doctors—the one for the medicine and the one she talked to—she might get worse, but she didn't. She had a purpose, you know?

"And then our baby was born. I sat there in the delivery room—me, I mean look at me. I'm probably not your dream of who's gonna be in the delivery room with your little girl some day, but there I was. And she was just so beautiful. They were both so beautiful. God, it was great.

"And we went home, and life was sweet. I worked overtime, as much as I could get, so we could have some more things. I'd come home, and they'd be asleep, my baby in her crib and my wife in our bed, and I thought, may be there is a heaven. Maybe there is a God.

"And now this. I mean, I live close to the water. I stayed on land, but I work with boats. It's harsh, man, real harsh. People die at sea—good ones and bad ones. Don't make no sense. And now this. Jesus Fucking H. Christ. It just don't make no sense. Those two in that room, they're the only thing that makes my life worth living every day, the only reason I get up every morning, and stay clean and sober, really, ya know. I mean, I want to go somewhere and say, take me. Not her. But I guess there's really nowhere to go, huh? There is no manager. Just us and all this.

"Anyway, I just wanted someone to know. And you're the one with the brain thing, so it kinda hinges on what you're gonna say. It's not like you're in charge of what happens, but you're sure as shit gonna be the messenger. And so I guess I thought you should know about us, a little, at least."

We sat in silence for a time.

"Thank you," I finally said. "I wish I could do more than

what I can do. But you're right, I'm not in charge. All I can promise is to tell you what I know, as soon as I know, and as much as I know. It is a harsh world we live in, and this place reminds me of that every time I pretend I don't know that fact. But we can keep each other company. That helps sometimes, I think."

He looked at me, unblinking and clear-eyed. "Yeah. It helps."

The days passed, and Rebecca's brain showed no signs of real recovery. All the information suggested her brain was badly injured, devastated. We did more tests, and they all pointed in the same direction. Her lungs and heart and kidneys and liver had recovered, but her brain functions had not. She needed the ventilator to support her breathing. Her EEG and scans showed a picture of the loss of all function that could allow her to live independently of machines.

We sat down again with Rebecca's parents, in that small room, and told them the situation. Rebecca's mother buried her head in the father's shoulder, and sobbed. Father stroked her head, and looked at us.

"We've talked about this, the two of us. We're pretty clear. We don't want to continue on, I mean, with all the machines and stuff, if she can't recover and be who she was going to be. We want to stop. Is that possible?"

Yes, we said, with this picture of complete loss of brain function, we could disconnect her from the machines that were keeping her artificially alive.

"And we want to donate whatever organs are okay? Is that possible?"

We must have looked surprised; organ donation from a dying infant is not usually something families bring up.

"I mean, we figure it this way, when we talk about it. Rebecca's life has to have a purpose, even as short as it was. Something good has to come out of all this bad. We can't save Rebecca, but she could help someone else's baby live. Isn't that what donating organs does?"

Yes, that is what organ donation does. We could look into this for them. It would change the way we organized things, but there were parts of her body that could be offered after she had been declared dead.

"That's okay. I mean, we want it this way," Rebecca's father said.

We agreed to look into this possibility, and left the family alone in the room.

"Houston, I think we have a problem," said the fellow as we left.

"This is a DA's call, isn't it?" asked the senior resident.

"Afraid so. Found dead at home, then resuscitated. Even if the organ bank finds something acceptable after a long anoxic injury—corneas, skin, we still have to get the district attorney to sign off on this as not being a suspicious death that they want to refer to the coroner."

"But the coroner never takes cases from here. They always say, 'It's a kid, get your pathologist to do the autopsy.' Couldn't we get the pathologist to pass over this one? Say there was no indication for autopsy in a case where organs are being donated? Or maybe do a partial post-mortem after organ harvest?"

"Not their call. The DA has to make the call."

The organ bank was notified of the situation and of the family's wishes, and a representative arrived quickly. Infant donors were few and far between, and the needs high.

The senior resident also told the family there was "one potential complicating factor," and explained about the legal situation. We would have to notify the district attorney, because of the law under these circumstances. They would also let the hospital attorney know, given this situation.

The family said they were ready to proceed, and Rebecca's breathing tube was removed. She was placed in her mother's arms. Her father hovered over the two of them, stroking first his daughter's hair, then his wife's. Rebecca's breathing was slow and irregular, and then stopped in a few minutes. Her heart stopped beating, and the senior resident declared her dead.

The fellow was on the phone at the nurse's station to the assistant district attorney on duty that day. I came away from the bedside, and she motioned me to get on another extension.

". . . afraid we'd have to call it a suspicious circumstance, and insist upon a post-mortem."

"How can you say that? This child died of complications of SIDS, and the family wants to donate whatever organs are possible."

"*Possible* SIDS, doctor. That is not yet proved. Once we have results of the post-mortem, I'll legally release the body and you can do whatever you want with it."

"This is not an experiment, sir. It's not what I want to do with the body. It is the wish of the dying child's parents. They want to help someone else's child."

"You're breaking my heart, doctor. It's a suspicious death, and I say no release until the autopsy."

"What is suspicious about this? It's tragic."

"Doctor, I ran the family's name. Father seems to be well known to the local police. A whole lot of appearances in our courts. I say it's a suspicious death, based on that record. I'm just doing my job, protecting the citizens of the commonwealth."

The fellow looked stunned. I motioned to her that I wanted to say something; she nodded.

I introduced myself.

"I wasn't aware there was anyone else on the line," said the ADA.

"I'm sorry; my fault for not saying anything. In any event, those arrests were years ago—there's nothing recent, correct?"

The shuffling of paper. " Yeah, so?"

"So that was then, and this is now. He's been out of trouble for years, got his life together, and now this happened. They just want to salvage some sense out of this whole thing; some kind of organ donation is what makes sense for them. If that's going to happen, it has to happen now. Calling for an autopsy makes that impossible."

"I'm sorry, really I am. But I cannot look at a situation with a dead child in a household with this many priors and not be diligent. It's my job."

"Look, if there had been any problem, wouldn't the Department of Social Services have been involved?"

"Yeah, right. I'm going to stake my job and my reputation on the DSS missing something? Or getting something right? Please, doc, I am not that stupid."

"So can't you trust our judgment? We've worked with this family for days now. This was a tragedy, and we're trying to help them and someone else this way."

"No way. Suspicious death, autopsy ordered, end of story. Call me when it's done and then I'll release the body."

"Too late."

"Not my problem, doctor. End of story."

The fellow and I looked at each other. Anger is an emotion with which I have long struggled—we are on close terms. I had enough presence of mind to know I needed to clear at least part of my mind of that destructive presence before we met again with Rebecca's parents. Lord Jesus Christ, Son of God, have mercy on me, a sinner, I prayed.

We met again with Rebecca's parents, and we told them what had just happened in as few words as possible. I thought that the fewer words I used, the less I might betray my own rage at the situation. I thought I might be more helpful to them if I could stay focused on them.

A silence, and then the father looked at me. Unblinking, and clear-eyed. "Pisses you off, too, du'n'it?"

I stammered, and spluttered, and then confessed. "Yes. It does."

"And not a thing we can do, is there. I mean, we got no connections, no friends that could make a call. They got me, dead to rights, for what I managed to escape before. I thought I got away, but I didn't. They'll get you in the end. If we'd been rich, even just well-off, this would be a made-for-TV movie. On that Lifetime channel or something. Brave, heroic family, making sense of their loss. But we're not that. We're trash. We're not supposed to be heroes. We're just supposed to do what we always do. Roll over. Play dead. Scrape by. Shit."

"I'm sorry. We tried to convince the assistant district attorney."

"I'm sure you did. Didn't work. That's it. Rebecca's dead and that's it."

"Can I do anything for you, now I mean?"

"No. We just need to be alone." He stared at the wall, his hand covering his wife's hands. She wept. We left.

We can think of compassion in a number of ways. We can think of it as trying to share another's sorrows, taking on some of their pain in an attempt to lighten their load. This kind of compassion, this suffering along with someone, has a kind of harsh solidarity in it. We choose to leave the path we are treading at a given moment, and walk in the path of another, often into harm's way in some form. Someone else is hurt, or suffering, or afflicted in some way, and we try to ease their pain by taking some of it on ourselves. In the Crucifixion story, the father of Rufus and Alexander shoulders the cross during the long, hard, sad walk to the place of the skull, and eases the burden of Jesus, in a very small way, for a very short time. That he is forced to do so by the authorities does not diminish the relief he provides to Jesus; for a brief period, someone else carries the cross. For Jesus—beaten, deprived of sleep, mocked, scorned—those few moments of relief must have been a mercy. From the perspective of Jesus, Simon the Cyrene's motivation is immaterial in that moment.

We can look on the piety of this type of compassion in several different ways. In part, there is an element of identification with the other. Another person has had something inflicted upon them, perhaps randomly, perhaps unjustly, perhaps without warning, and stumbles under this assault. Their life, their balance, has been upset by this painful event. Literally or not, they trip. We rush forward, even though the issue is not ours, and we claim part of it as ours. This is not our loss, our pain, our sadness, but we take on a part of it. Showing compassion in this way is an act of acknowledging our profound attachment to the person in pain. We may be forced into this act of sharing by the authority of the state, by the circumstances of our job or position, by the expectations of those around us, or we may do it from what seems to be pure free will. The human heart is a complicated, contrary place. The relief the other feels in the moment of our taking on some part of their pain is, at one level, uninfluenced by the matter of our intent or lack of it.

This aspect of compassion, one person taking the place—for a time and in part—for another in the midst of their pain, ultimately forces us to acknowledge our deep connections. You and I are not the same person, your pain and loss are very much particular to you, but for a moment I will take it on. In this act of taking on, I make manifest our deep connection. We may be related by ties of blood or affection, or we may never have met before this moment. We may have a relationship that is complex and troubled, or deeply loving and profoundly supportive. We may be strangers on a crowded street, soldiers on a battlefield, people caught up in the chaos of a natural disaster, or a nurse and a patient in an emergency room. Wherever we are, whoever we are, if one of us takes on part of the burdens of the other, we have made incarnate, in the flesh, our acceptance of some deep tie that binds us. To suffer along with someone is to acknowledge a common humanity that transcends whatever categories we use to define ourselves from day to day.

This kind of compassion, suffering along with someone, is subversive for this very fact: for a moment, everything that divides us is overcome by what unites us. All the authorities of this world which seek to oppress us, to inflict fear and damage and pain upon us, depend upon our divisions. My engagement in your oppression is dependent upon my definition of myself as somehow different from you. When you show compassion for me by taking part of my burden, my pain, my suffering, my loss, you have overcome, even for the smallest of moments, that chasm which divides us. Rich or poor, man or woman, friend or enemy, those definitions are undermined by this element of compassion.

This solidarity with the suffering of another—made incarnate, made physical, by taking on another's loss—erodes the foundations of oppression. Whatever gulf has separated us has been bridged, even if only for a short time, and both hearts cannot engage quite so freely, quite so gleefully, in making someone else's differences the object of scorn or fear. The authorities that would stay in control need us all to be fearful of one another, to dwell upon our differences rather than our connections, to think of ourselves first and others, whoever they may be, as little as possible.

Compassion flies in the face of this oppressive and divisive authority. Compassion of this type says that your self-interest is not all there is to life, that your small comforts and pleasures, or your very safety itself, can be set aside for someone else's needs. The purchase, the hold that the authorities have by constantly whispering in your ear that this life is limited, a zero-sum game, that whatever you have must be jealously hoarded and guarded, is subverted by acts of compassion. You say, in essence, that in this moment you will risk what you have and what you are, so that you may help another. You will take something painful, ugly, or hurtful that was not yours, and make it yours, even for a moment, so that someone else may have some small measure of ease and comfort. In so doing, you say to the authorities that their reign of fear and subjection has its limits, and that you choose to transcend them. You say that jealous protection of your own being is not the law of your life—at least not at this particular moment. You say to the authorities that this person's pain is not primarily understood as a sociopolitical fact, or as a consequence of their bad choices, or as a place in a social stratum into which you fear falling. You say that this person's pain and loss are primarily understood as your problem because you are deeply connected to them.

For example, the fact that someone has HIV/AIDS can be delineated as a series of biological facts—method of transmission, choices that led to the infection, failure to engage in various forms of preventive behaviors. If we leave the situation at that, then the authorities of this world allow us to look at a person with HIV/AIDS and measure our response to that person accordingly: bad choices, poor habits, too bad. Not my problem. Compassion extends our view beyond the sad facts of biology and politics. Compassion insists upon a solidarity with the person with HIV/AIDS, a solidarity that transcends whatever categories are used to separate us. Compassion insists that nothing is more important than the pain of another person because that other person is profoundly, intimately, deeply connected to us through our common incarnation. Nothing—not patent laws that protect the exclusive ownership of medications by the companies that market them, not budgetary decisions that determine which sort of relief activities are funded and which are not, not derived principles of which victims have warranted our help because they have changed their behavior as we would like—nothing supersedes this type of compassion. This vision of compassion is a profoundly subversive notion.

Compassion as the experienced sharing of another's burdens chips away at the foundations of worldly authority by undermining all its dearest principles. Compassion looks at private property and says that its rights are limited under certain conditions. If a quarter of the population is suffering from an illness for which treatment exists, compassion demands that this treatment be made available now, and not after careful studies or agreements have been brokered. Compassion looks at the law and says that when a law is unjust and oppressive, it must be broken before it is rewritten. Compassion looks at authority and says that when authority becomes institutionalized violence, it must be confronted before it is reformed. Compassion says that if sub-Saharan Africa is afflicted by HIV/AIDS, then I am affected by HIV/AIDS, and I must demand that treatment be made available. If those who control the medications that can save lives will not make them readily available, then I will work for making them available and plentiful by whatever means is necessary. Not the customs of private property, not the laws created by the authorities of the rich, not the protection of those privileges by legions of police and army have final authority in the face of an act of compassion. An act of compassion subverts all this authority for a startling notion—we are all connected through the common fact of our incarnation, our physical beings. The recognition of this commonality is the basis for a profound solidarity. Authority depends upon our divisions; compassion speaks to our unity.

Yet this kind of compassion also frightens us because we worry that it will deplete us. By giving of ourselves, we worry that we will have nothing left over. We worry about burn-out, exhaustion. We may have experienced this exhaustion ourselves, or watched it happen to someone we know. We may have been raised in a household where the adults gave so much of themselves during the workday that there seemed to be nothing left over for us when they finally came home. If those who raised us were teachers, police officers, firefighters, members of the clergy, or health care providers, we may have memories of a compassion that seemed to steal from us. We may feel that our parents had nothing left over to give us at the end of a long day because they had given it all away in the context of their vocation.

Or we may have had the experience ourselves. We may have thrown all our energies into caring for someone or something, and found that after a time we felt tapped out, with nothing to offer those whom we loved the most. This kind of compassion for others may have felt unfair to those we loved. It may have led to conflict or shattered relationships. It may have led to estrangement or divorce. How can this be what we are meant to do?

I think the problem with this understanding of compassion is its limited view. We are meant to have a radical identification with as many of our brothers and sisters as we can muster. We are meant to clothe the naked, feed the hungry, care for the widow and orphan. How much better our collective life as communities of faith would be if we were to replace the dry theology of the Nicene Creed with a weekly recitation of the Beatitudes! Or with the even starker reminder of Jesus' summary of all the law and all the prophets: We are to love God with all our heart, all our soul, all our mind, all our strength. With all that we are, we are to plunge into dizzying, headlong devotion. And then, we are to love everyone we encounter, and everyone we will never encounter, as we love ourselves. An appallingly simple set of commands.

Yet how can we possibly live up to this challenge without feeling exhausted? How can we manifest this kind of compassion without ending up spent? How can we avoid the pinched and narrow piety of a life that constantly measures how much we give by how little we have left for ourselves? How can this be any sort of a joyous life? I think an answer lies in the source of our compassion.

We are not meant to engage in these mighty deeds of power alone or with only our own resources. The compassion we manifest as part of our incarnation derives not from our own very limited minds and hearts, but from our nature as images of the divine. God is present in the space between me and another when we engage in compassion, when our hearts give expression to this radical and inclusive lovingkindness. If God is love, then giving that love shape and form, heft and substance, through an act of compassion will then allow both individuals involved to serve as conduits, as vessels of that divine love. We are no longer dependent upon our own limited understanding, our own finite resources, our own narrow vision. When we engage in an act of compassion, when we surrender even a part of our heart to such an act, we then enter the infinite stream of divine love.

That stream, that river, existed before time began, and it will continue to the end of time. That stream is inexhaustible, it never fails. When we choose to allow the stream of divine love to flow through us, even for a moment, even only in part, we become part of the divine. We claim our heritage as sons and daughters of God. We become vessels of the divine love. We burn, but are not consumed.

And this rootedness in the divine, this statement through our lives of our true natures, this participation in boundless compassion and endless lovingkindness, is profoundly subversive. It is subversive because it is fearless—whatever happens, to us or another, we live and die in the embrace of this stunning love that is the warp and woof of the universe. It is subversive because it occupies all the space in our hearts and minds that would otherwise be taken by the niggling fears and doubts that separate us from our better natures, our true natures, and from each other. If we live and abide in this love, then the tawdry fictions that empires use to divide us from one another have no hold on our hearts. If we live and abide in this love, we can see anyone we encounter only as our brother or our sister; categories such as friend, enemy, competitor, and, rival become meaningless. We can only desire what is best for everyone we encounter. I desire for everyone I encounter the same blessings, gifts, and privileges I would want for my own children, my own spouse, my own siblings.

Empires are always built on foundations of sand. Their

machinery of oppression is never as powerful as it seems; it only functions because those whom it attempts to subjugate are divided. Empires divide us by class, race, sexual orientation, religion, gender, physical attributes, or intelligence. By giving minor privileges to some, and withholding those privileges from others, they keep us all divided. Those of us with privileges worry that we will somehow lose this pittance we have been given, and fall into the pit in which the others have been cast. When we engage in acts of compassion, we render those divisions irrelevant in two ways: First, we say that they are not categories we accept or acknowledge as legitimate, and that our common incarnation as human is the only category we accept as valid. Second, by diving headlong, deliriously, openly into the stream of lovingkindness and compassion that lies at the heart of the universe, we reject the very power of the empire as small, paltry, and of little long-term consequence. Whatever empire we encounter, we place it in the sad procession of other empires that have come and gone, forgotten and in ruins.

Months after baby Rebecca's death, I saw her father again. I asked how he and his wife were doing.

"We're doing okay. We're doing okay. My wife was back in the hospital for a while, but she's better now."

I told Rebecca's father that I was sorry that there was nothing I seemed to have been able to do to help them in their wish for their daughter.

"No, you're wrong there."

I blushed, thinking he was about to take me to task, suggesting that I could have somehow mustered more effective intervention with the DA's office. I had felt guilty and angry about this for quite a long time.

"You're wrong because it did help. This is a harsh world we live in, when little babies die in their sleep. All of you here at the hospital tried the best you could, and we appreciate that.

This is the best place we could have been with Rebecca, and so we can sort of learn to live with her dying a little easier because of that.

"But the really important thing was this: We wanted to donate her organs, and you took that seriously. We made a choice, it's like we took a stand, and you were there with us when we did. It didn't work out in the end, but we made our choice. We said, we are here and here is what we want to do. And it kinda felt like you were there beside us. Like you said, we're here, too. It didn't work out, the DA kinda won. Only he didn't really. Because we said what we wanted to do, and they can't take that away. And you noticed it, and accepted it. Supported it, like. We were left standing. Maybe that's all it can be. But we wanted to offer something, and the offer was accepted. By you—all of you. And that meant we were like on the same level. And that felt okay."

The machinery of the Roman occupation of Palestine two thousand years ago is long gone. Ruined fortresses, a handful of names, and some documents are all that remain. The Romans' accomplices and collaborators have also disappeared, mostly forgotten. Such are the wages of empire. The Republic of the United States of America and the Commonwealth of Massachusetts will also disappear someday. The decisions of the district attorney's office, perhaps even the names of its personnel, may survive in some obscure library somewhere; perhaps scholars of another succeeding state will study them, and perhaps not. If experience and history have taught us anything, it is that all the fevered imaginings and desires of empire builders eventually fade away to dust and memories.

On the other hand, the mighty deeds of power that taught a community of marginalized hill folk that their lives had dignity and meaning, that the kingdom of God was constantly being created by them through acts of compassion—these mighty acts of power—still have life. They exist in an unbroken chain, across time and space. The stream from which those acts arose, the deep compassion and boundless lovingkindness that illuminated those acts, is in direct connection with the world in which we live and move and have our being today. That stream flows through us as it flowed through them, and it carries us all along. When we engage in such acts of power, when we show true compassion for one another, the space between any two of us becomes the kingdom of God, and is filled with God. And the kingdom of God subverts all the powers of this world that would corrupt and destroy the children of God. When we surrender to this compassion and lovingkindness, we partake of a life that is ordered according to the dream of God. When we incarnate compassion, and live to each other and for each other in the full measure of our identity as nothing but the children of God, we then live in the kingdom of God. No empire has ever been able to stand before this power, and none ever will.

HEALING AS A POLITICAL ACT

⎯⫙⎯

During my medical training, I spent a year as house officer in internal medicine at the old Peter Bent Brigham Hospital in Boston, now long merged into a series of successor institutions. My advisor in medical school had heard me speak of my desire to become a pediatric neurologist, but felt that the intellectual discipline of at least a year in internal medicine would be helpful. "Pediatricians are a bit woofty," he said, "a bit too Mr. Rogers. You won't ever think well if you don't start out in internal medicine." Being who I was, and the times being what they were, such advice was taken as if from on high. I found myself in one of Harvard's teaching hospitals, taking care of adults, or, as I called them, given my affinities, "grown-ups."

Part of our rotations as interns was through the oncology inpatient service at the Dana Farber Cancer Institute across the street. The patients there were all hospitalized for various chemotherapy protocols, prescribed sequences of treatments for various forms of cancer. Most patients came there because they were ill with forms of cancer that had not responded to conventional treatments, or were not likely to do so. These patients were profoundly ill. We interns admitted the cancer patients to the hospital, and wrote orders for the complicated regimens of medications prescribed by the attending physicians and fellows. We had to know the side effects each of these drugs might produce, and watch out for them in our patients. We did not do much thinking or learning about the treatment of cancer; our job was mostly to do the "scut," the day-to-day tasks that made the hospital function. We started intravenous lines in people who had had hundreds of these lines placed and in whom, as a result, suitable veins were now hard to find. We evaluated people for high fevers when their immune systems were suppressed by chemotherapy or radiation and the source of infection was unclear. We ordered anti-nausea medications for people who threw up everything in their guts and then kept puking. This was the era of the "War on Cancer" declared by the federal government. We interns were the infantry. "Your job isn't to think," one of my fellows said in a candid moment, "it's just to work and do what I tell you."

In this rotation, we were on call every third night, which was less frequently than during many other parts of our year. The institute had no emergency room of its own that we had to staff; patients arrived from other ERs or doctors' offices. The rotation was referred to as a "country club" experience because of these two facts. I settled in reasonably well, having given up any notion of independent thought in exchange for a little more sleep and a clear chain of command.

I inherited a group of my patients from one of my fellow interns when I arrived. He was moving on to another service; I was coming from another service to take his place. At that time, most of the patients were finishing a protocol and would leave in a day or two. I would have to dictate the discharge summaries, since they would leave the hospital on my watch. I was grateful to see that my predecessor had left fairly complete summaries of the patients' treatments as "off-service notes." On my first day, we walked around the ward, and he introduced me to the patients.

Before we went into one room, he said, "This guy's here for the duration. Nowhere to go, and no one to take him there. Head-and-neck cancer. Truly disgusting weeping wound in his neck. Your job is to go in every day and dress the wound along with the nurse. It's pretty rude." He opened the door, and a powerful odor wafted out. He stuck his head inside the door, and waved to a man who looked far older than his actual age of 63, lying on the bed with a large dressing around his neck, like a big gauze turtleneck.

"Hey there, Norman. This is your new intern, Dr. Urion. He'll be coming around tomorrow. Everything okay? Good."

I started to walk into the room, and bumped into my predecessor backing out as he closed the door. For all the other patients, I had been shown their most salient physical findings on exam, or we had spent some time meeting and talking with my new charges. I could see that my predecessor tried, quite successfully, to avoid any contact, conversational or otherwise, that would have required entering Norman's room.

The next morning I came in to "pre-round" on my patients: to find out what had happened overnight, look up their laboratory studies, and generally get ready for the walk rounds we would do with the rest of the team. At that time, I would be expected to know all the particulars of each patient's case, and to express a plan formulated for the day, with special attention to areas of concern: urine output for people on chemotherapy (which could damage the kidneys), blood-cell counts for people who had just received chemotherapy, and chest X-ray results. When I stepped into Norman's room, he smiled. He could not talk, but gestured hello. The smell from Norman's wound was quite astonishing, even through all the layers of gauze. I tried to close my nostrils as I listened to his heart and lungs. I told him I'd be back mid-morning with the nurse to change the dressing on his wound.

On rounds, the group stopped by Norman's door. Typically during rounds, the intern first recounted the news, the "counts and amounts," and then led the team in. He (in those days still usually a he) would then demonstrate the physical findings of note, the senior resident would verify these findings, a few words would be said to the patient, and then we would walk out into the hallway. Discussion would ensue.

I recounted the few facts about Norman from the night before, and then began to open his door.

"No need," said my senior resident, pulling it closed again.
Then he rattled off what everyone already knew: "Headand
neckcancerinaformersmoker. Failed chemo times two, now
has suppurating wound in neck that will not close. No family
or friends to take him in. He'll either get an overwhelming infection from his open wound and die, or erode through some
vital structure such as carotid artery, trachea, or esophagus
and die. I assume you would have told us if any of these things
had come to pass, Dr. Urion. He's still our guest at Medicaid
rates. Let's move on."

Later that morning, I went to find Norman's nurse. Interns
were assigned to patients, but nurses on this unit were allowed
to choose their patients if they had sufficient seniority. Most
of Norman's nurses were very junior, new kids on the block;
he was not viewed as a desirable patient. I was a bit worried
about this, not because of what it told me about his place in
the social order of the unit, but because I didn't think of myself as very adept at wound care. One junior nurse and one
inept intern trying to dress such a wound could make a hash
of it. I had visions of injuring Norman's carotid artery when I
tried to change the dressing—I imagined the artery swimming
in the wound before me when I took off the old gauze. Only
one senior nurse had volunteered to be on Norman's care
team. As luck would have it, she was on that day.

This particular nurse was somewhat notorious on the unit,
at least among the house officers. She was reputed to be a
woman of what my grandfather would have called "easy virtue," although I suspect the evidence supporting this reputation was thin and overinterpreted by a group of men in the
prolonged adolescent-fratboy atmosphere of a teaching hospital. She was certainly beautiful, and was thoroughly unim-
pressed by my doctorate.

"Ever done this before? I didn't think so. Just watch me,

okay? And hand me what I ask for. After a few days, you'll probably get good enough that I'll let you do it. The new grads will think you're wonderful. Hold these." She handed me bottles of iodine solution, hydrogen peroxide, antibiotic cream, saline solution. Miles of gauze, dressings. We went in.

The nurse's face immediately changed—it lit up. "Hello, handsome. You met your new intern, didn't you? I'm going to help him change your dressing. Did you get enough percocet? Feeling okay?" Norman smiled, a bit dreamily. We put on gloves.

She pointed to the dressing as she turned Norman's head to the side. He was facing away from his wound. "Saline there, Dr. Urion?" The question created the auditory illusion that she was asking for instruction instead of giving it. I wet the dressing.

After peeling the saturated gauze off, the wound could be smelled before it was seen. The stench in the room became something you could taste on the air. The wound sat there in the side of the neck, a large, oval crater. The sides were oozing a grey-green viscous liquid, and islands of pink granulation tissue could be seen in a few spots. At the bottom were several long hummocks that ran the length of the wound. They were the carotid artery, the trachea, and the jugular vein, all barely covered by a thin layer of tissue the cancer had not yet consumed.

"Should we clean this up with peroxide first?" Her questions led me through all the phases of the ballet. I finished by wrapping the gauze around the bandage that covered the hole, as the nurse held up Norman's head, gently, lovingly. "There, done."

Norman smiled at her, looked at me, and mouthed, "Thanks." She stayed to arrange his bedclothes. I took the old dressing materials and gloves, and threw them in the large red can marked "infectious waste."

"Not bad," she said later at the nurse's station. "Most of the others gag when they take the dressing off the first time."

"A bit like not getting seasick—I can't claim any moral superiority."

She laughed, "That's funny."

"It's Mark Twain."

"And you're honest."

"It seems so sad. I mean, dying alone like that. No family, no friends. The wages of sin, I guess."

"What?"

"Smoking. That's how he got his cancer, right? And now that's how it comes home to roost. Alone in a hospital room, waiting to die, taken care of by strangers."

"What do you know about him? What do you know that gives you the right to say that?" She turned on her heel and walked away.

Care always exists in a context. We are cared for in the setting of relationships—couples, families, classrooms, communities, doctors and patients. Those relationships bring along with them various attributes—boundaries, histories, assumptions. When those attributes vary from the norm we have come to expect in a given context, we feel uncomfortable at the least, violated at the worst. For example, we expect helpless infants to be cared for in a certain fashion by their parent or parents. The complete dependence of a newborn on the adults around him or her creates a powerful set of social expectations that the infants' basic needs be met. Parents who cannot or will not provide such care will see their relationship with that newborn infant altered, as other adult members of the community step in. Depending upon the culture and situation, someone else will usually sweep in and take over, restore the order we expect to exist in the life of an infant. Nourishment will be provided, diapers will be changed, shelter and warmth will be ensured. This may be done by a senior relative, a village elder, or the forces of the social service agencies of the state, but the mores of human society in this regard are fairly universal. We are, in a profound sense, programmed to make certain that infants receive the care they need, and parents who do not or cannot succeed in providing this care will have their autonomy put aside and their authority usurped.

This process is, in the end, a kind of political decision. The constituted body of society, the *polis* in the classic Greek term, has a set of values which are bedrock, which cannot be denied or ignored. When members of the *polis* violate those norms, they lose part of their membership in that society. It is not acceptable to any functioning human society that a helpless infant be left unattended, unwashed, and unfed, and so all human societies have some mechanism that will intervene if such neglect is discovered. Societies that fail to provide such surveillance are profoundly dysfunctional, often on the verge of collapse as recognizably human.

The Gospel of Mark describes a society that is hard pressed. The society, the functional *polis* at the center of Mark's gospel, is the marginalized Jewish community of Galilee. It constitutes what has been called the "little tradition" in Palestine of that era, to contrast it with the "big tradition" of Jerusalem and the Temple. The society in which Jesus is portrayed throughout Mark is rural, poor, by and large not literate, and quite powerless. It was subject to confiscatory taxes, both to the occupying Roman forces, as well as the collaborationist Jewish authorities. Its religious life was led by teachers, rabbis in synagogues, and not by the priestly caste of the Temple. Its daily political and religious autonomy had been eroded by the incursions of these Roman and big-tradition forces, and any prosperity it had known had been destroyed by the economic policies of imperial Rome in its provinces. It lacked both fiscal and social capital.

And it was restless. We know from Mark's gospel, as well as other historic documents of the time, that movements arose among these hill folk that pushed back against Roman and Temple oppression. The countryside swarmed with itinerant teachers, miracle workers, prophets, and irregular military guerrilla leaders, all of whom had transient followings and fluid programs and agendas. Depending upon your vantage point, these teachers could be seen as inspired or as dangerously unorthodox; these miracle workers could be considered holy men or charlatans; these prophets could be known as wise men calling for God's justice or as crackpots stirring up trouble; these guerrilla leaders could be portrayed as noble warriors or as outlaws. Most were probably volatile mixtures of all of these qualities.

The Jesus of Mark's gospel exists in this context. He arises from these people, and his ministry is first to them. He wanders the hillsides and roads of Galilee, rows across its sea, preaches in its synagogues and open spaces, retreats into its wilderness, and sits in its village squares. He is very much a product of this world.

His teaching and preaching are rooted in the context of these lives he knows so well. His metaphors are not obscure to this audience; he does not baffle them with learned subtleties or elegant theology. He speaks of things they know: mustard seeds and oil lamps, salt and sea and waves, harvests and catches, ingrate sons and haughty rich folk. This is the language of a poor people in an occupied country who still harbor high dreams.

Jesus speaks to them of a kingdom in the midst of imperial occupation. He speaks of restoring a set of right relationships between people, of aligning Galilean society with God's dream for the world. He acknowledges the existence of the Roman authorities, and looks foursquare at the authority of the Temple. Yet amid these harsh realities, he asks his audience to imagine a new set of relationships, a new society, a new kingdom, coming into being right under the noses of the oppressors. He imagines a profound reconstruction of the world through an audacious reforming of the human heart. The kingdom of God is very near, his listeners are constantly told. It is not in some future time, or after some future event, but here and now—if they but grasp it, see it, live into it.

In the Gospel of Mark, Jesus' fundamental means of demonstrating what this kingdom is—not what it will look like at some millennial moment, but what it is at this very moment—are his healing acts of power. These healing acts are not isolated acts of individual restoration. Jesus does not set about to establish the All Palestine Campaign to Eradicate Leprosy or the Galilean Initiative against Blindness, although the stories all demonstrate a deep, profound, and gentle compassion for the individuals he heals. Each of these healing acts of power demonstrates the incorporation, the integration, the *re-membering* of some marginalized part of the community. This is what the kingdom is: the radical inclusion of all in the community. Hearts that can accept the lame, the blind, the leprous, and the paralyzed as full members of the community are hearts that are open and full of boundless compassion. Hearts so reformed, remade in this image, are in and of themselves the necessary and sufficient conditions for the kingdom of God.

In the Gospel of Mark, Jesus is portrayed as someone who sets out to create a radically new community, one deeply rooted. This community, which he insists in calling the kingdom of God, has certain attributes of which he speaks incessantly. It is emphatically in the present moment: we are told, the audience is told, that the kingdom of God is very near to you. Not in some far-off time, not after some triumph over the political authorities of the day, not after some millennial moment. The Jesus portrayed in Mark speaks constantly of a kingdom of God being in the present moment. In this way, he redefines the arguments of his time. When would the Messiah come? When would the Temple be restored? When would the people of God see their enemies subdued and their lots in life restored? The Jesus portrayed in Mark says that this restoration is already happening. It occurs now, in reformed human hearts.

The Jesus portrayed in Mark also insists that this kingdom of God is being established where he is with his followers. That is, the kingdom of God is not only now, it is here, the Gospel of Mark says. Far from the apparent political authority of the day represented by Rome and its procurators and legions, far from the spiritual authority of the day represented by the priestly caste in Jerusalem. The kingdom of God is making its appearance among this downcast, lowly people. The kingdom of God is appearing among the marginalized and the poor. The kingdom of God, the Gospel of Mark insists, is appearing before your very eyes and ears.

The Jesus portrayed in Mark establishes this kingdom by means that surprise and mystify his followers, even those closest to him. He claims his authority and establishes the kingdom of God through his mighty acts of power among, and for the benefit of, this outcast people. That is, he establishes the kingdom of God by providing a model. The kingdom of God will exist not through strength of military might, not through piety, not through scrupulous attention to the Law, and not through the appropriation of the seat of religious authority. The kingdom of God is established when all the members of the people of God are included in the loving embrace of God made manifest through the people—and that includes a man on Medicaid dying alone of cancer with an outrageously putrid neck wound.

Jesus reminds his followers time and again that God is love, that they are accepted and welcomed into God's enormous and compassionate fold by their very nature. Jesus reminds his followers that God is constantly approaching them, desiring them, longing for them. His model of the kingdom of God is this: to embrace one another in the same way that God embraces each and every member of the community. The kingdom of God will be established in the here and the now when every member of the community is accepted with the same eyes of profound love with which God accepts every person.

The mighty acts of power that heal people's infirmities are meant to serve as a model of that love. It is not the act of physical restoration that brings about the kingdom of God. It is the taking of one outcast member and bringing him or her back into community. It is the expending of Jesus' extraordinary power on the ill, the halt, and the lame that serves as the exemplar of how we are to act.

Jesus has been given power; we know this and hear this throughout the Gospel of Mark. The story begins with no birth narrative, no recounting of lineage. We are told instead that it is "the beginning of the good news of Jesus Christ, the Son of God" (Mark 1:1). The story then plunges into the appearance of John the baptizer, one of the many wild and holy men who populated the countryside of Galilee. John rambles the countryside, preaching repentance, speaking of the deep longing of this people for a restoration of their community as the beloved people of God. Into the midst of this gathering, Jesus appears as a grown man. He is baptized, an act which gives John pause. Jesus emerges from the water, and his nature is revealed. Jesus sees the heavens part and the Spirit of God descending upon him. All then hear a voice, declaring Jesus to be the Son of God, the Beloved, in whom God is well pleased. His power is established, his identity and authority made clear.

Jesus could have done any number of things with his power. His first response, after his baptism, is to go into the wilderness, where Mark tells us only that he was tempted, tempted by Satan. How? To do what? Mark is silent on these matters, telling us only that angels attend Jesus during his trials.

Yet we soon get some insight into what Jesus has decided to do with this power, this authority, when John is arrested, and Jesus returns to Galilee. He proclaims "the good news of God," saying "The time is fulfilled, and the kingdom of God has come near, repent, and believe in the good news" (Mark 1:14–15).

Jesus, his identity and authority revealed through his immersion in a people's repentance movement, first disappears into the wilderness, then returns to Galilee. His baptism demonstrates his complete solidarity with the people from whom he arose. His return to those same people, after his time of temptation and contemplation in the wilderness, shows that this proclaiming of the good news is first and foremost for the people of God who have not been included in the constructs of power of the day. The community to which he will preach, in which he will move, for which he will perform mighty acts of power, is the community of Galilee.

The kingdom of God will be revealed among a certain people, at a certain time. This community has specific characteristics—beliefs, values, history, and memory. The timeless immediacy of the kingdom, the utterly egalitarian notions of its membership, will be revealed in a very specific community, of a very specific time, and with a very specific membership. The kingdom of God as it is revealed is thus present in a political community; it is not, however, as we are to learn, limited to that political community.

Jesus confronts this community, again and again, through his mighty acts of power that heal. These acts of power restore people to the community because the community has shunned them. People with unclean spirits, thought to be demonically possessed, are brought back into the community. Their demonic nature is revealed to be overcome by the touch of love and compassion through the Beloved one, the Son of God. Their exclusion, not their nature, is revealed to be demonic. People who manifest various forms of disease thought to be signs of divine disfavor—leprosy, paralysis, blindness, deaf-mutism, epilepsy—are returned to the community. Their afflictions are removed from them, but the real affliction is always shown to be the *community's* paralysis, the *community's* blindness, the *community's* deafness and failure to speak. Each of these persons is shown to be completely lovely in Jesus' sight and touch; once they are seen by him in that fashion, they are accepted as such by the community and restored. In each of these acts of healing, the community itself is healed because a missing member has been returned.

Jesus' healing is a political act because it dictates one of the primary aspects of life as a political community—the question of who is a member. Communities can determine their membership by a number of means. You might be a member of a community because you were born into it. Membership in the community in Galilee, for example, was based on lineage and birth. You can be a member of a community because you subscribe to certain beliefs and values. The community in Galilee lived by a version of the Law, as their own leadership and the leadership in Jerusalem interpreted it; certain people put themselves outside that fellowship, that community, by their actions and were viewed as unclean. Other people were put outside that community because of facts or aspects of their lives that were interpreted as the mark of uncleanness, of being outside the law—lepers, for example, whose identity we know was determined by biology, were viewed as outside the boundaries of the community. Other people had their status in the community diminished because of their natures—the paralyzed, the blind, the deaf.

Jesus takes all these definitions, all these boundaries, all these delineations of the community as a defined, prescribing and proscribing body, and reforms them. He reminds the community that it is the people of God, and that their life together is the very kingdom of God, whenever and wherever the wholeness of the people of God is restored. Whenever a member who had been forced out is returned, then the kingdom of is God very near. Whenever those whom God has embraced and loved since before time and space began are recognized—at a specific time and place—as part of the community, at that moment the community becomes the kingdom of God.

What Jesus models is a radical redefinition of the community. It is a community in which there are no outcasts, one in which all the ways that people have used to distinguish themselves from one another are rendered irrelevant. God smiles on people by their nature as people, no more and no less. Our failure to recognize any other human being as God's beloved makes us ungodly. Our prowess, our abilities, our strength, our wisdom, our sight, our hearing—all of these can be used by God and the community, all of these can be honored, all of them can be cherished. They cannot be used, however, to establish membership in the community, that is, member-ship in the kingdom. That membership is established solely by our being human and therefore beloved of God. Jesus uses his mighty acts of power time and again to remind the com-munity of this radical acceptance. The acts of power which restore health to the individual are used more importantly to restore health to the community because they reincorporate that community.

At the end of one day at the cancer institute, I was making my evening rounds. I walked into each patient's room, made certain that everything I should have done that day had been done, that all my patients were as stable as sick people with cancer could be, before handing responsibility for their care over to the intern on call that night.

When I walked into Norman's room, the lights were low, and it took some time for my eyes to adjust. I saw that his nurse was sitting at his bedside, holding his hand. I started to say something, trying to find some words to apologize for how my harshness had offended her earlier that day, but she put her index finger to her lips, and motioned with her head to Norman. He was, it seemed, drifting off to sleep. Her gestures and position reminded me a mother settling her child to sleep.

The most beautiful jazz I had ever heard was drifting through the room, from a tape player. I had grown up listen-ing to a lot of jazz, since my father and uncle had briefly been professionals, and had stayed avid amateurs. This music was wonderful—a saxophone, playing slow, sweet, heartbreakingly sad music. It conjured up wet sidewalks, smoky rooms, late hours. It was the music of lost loves and lost chances.

Norman had fallen asleep.

"That's him playing, you know," the nurse whispered. "He was one of the best, they say. Some of his old friends used to come by—they told me that. They don't come much, anymore. It must be hard to see him like this.

"They say cancer is the honorable jazzman's death. Otherwise, it's usually cirrhosis. It's hard to think of this as an honor.

"He wrote this music for his daughter. He hasn't seen her in years. She's never come by."

"It's beautiful," I said.

"*He's* beautiful," she said, looking down at Norman, and stroking his forehead with her free hand.

I stood, and she sat, holding his hand for a while. I asked if there was anything else he needed for the night.

"No. He's fine."

A few weeks later, I came into Norman's room and it was empty. I found the intern who had been on call the night before, and I asked what had happened.

"Jesus, Mary, and Joseph, man, you wouldn't believe it. Bled out. The cancer finally rotted away to the carotid, and he bled out. All over the room. Big red. Worst frickin' thing I've ever seen. Hit the walls, ceiling, everything. At least it must have been fast. You gonna do the discharge summary, man?"

"What? Yeah, I'll do the d.c."

I found Norman's nurse at the desk.

"I'm sorry," I said.

Her eyes were red. "Yeah, well, don't be. It's sad, but not sorry. He's at peace."

"You gave him a good end. No one wanted to take care of him, and you did. I mean, the wound and the smell and all. It was hard to take care of him. I know it meant a lot to him, what you did. Always so nice and kind."

She looked surprised. "It was easy. He was so beautiful. He had such a beautiful soul."

The kingdom of God was very near.

2

The Deeds of Power: Encounters

The author of the Gospel of Mark wants us to understand the nature of the kingdom of God. Some contemporary scholars hypothesize that the gospel was originally an oral narrative, a sort of theatrical reading, of the life and ministry of Jesus. What it lacks—a birth narrative, the story of Jesus' childhood—tells us something about its intended message. This was a story about community—how it is called, how it is built, what its attributes might be. In addition, it was a story *for* a specific community, the people of Galilee, the "little tradition"—a community that was rural, poor, oppressed by the forces of the Roman Empire as well as by the forces of the "big tradition" in the Temple in Jerusalem. The narrative, therefore, has a propulsive immediacy about the life the people of Galilee led, and the kind of life they were being called to lead.

The Gospel of Mark is told in a spare, focused style. The narrative centers around the teachings of Jesus about community, and how the people of God can participate in the kingdom of God—not someday, or somewhere, but right in the midst of their lives. The narrative is thus a roadmap, a set of directions, for how a people can participate with God in bringing about this jubilee.

The author of Mark's gospel tells the story of Jesus in a way that the community of Galilee can fathom. The Scriptures cited in Mark would have been familiar to this community—texts they had heard many times before—but now revealed in a new context with astonishing power. The stories that Jesus tells in this gospel use the commonalities of their daily lives, not arcane theological teachings, to make their points: mustard seeds and fields, vineyards and agricultural laborers, taxes and cruel masters. The deeds of power Jesus performs also occur in the midst of the daily lives these people lead. The people he heals—the blind, the lame, the possessed, the leprous—all these are in plain view, and in plain need.

In the following pages, I reflect on these stories, and connect them with events that I have experienced. The stories, after all, would have had the ring of everyday life to the people who first heard them. I invite you to recapture that immediacy by placing them in contexts familiar to us today. The context in which I have best understood these deeds of power is in the lives of families and children I have known.

THE MAN WITH THE UNCLEAN SPIRIT

What Does the Face of Love Look Like?

—Ⅲ—

They went to Capernaum, and when the Sabbath
came, he entered the synagogue and taught. They were
astounded at his teaching, for he taught them as one
having authority, and not as the scribes. Just then there
was in their synagogue a man with an unclean spirit,
and he cried out, "What have you to do with us, Jesus of
Nazareth? Have you come to destroy us? I know who
you are, the Holy One of God." But Jesus rebuked him,
saying, "Be silent, and come out of him!" And the unclean spirit, convulsing him and crying with a loud voice,
came out of him. They were all amazed, and they kept
on asking one another, "What is this? A new teaching—
with authority! He commands even the unclean spirits,
and they obey him."

Mark 1:21–27

I once took care of Renee, a little girl who had experienced
a cardiac arrest. She had been resuscitated, but after a fairly
long period of her brain being deprived of blood and oxygen.
As a result, Renee had been left with rather significant neurological difficulties. She had to negotiate life in a wheelchair,
she needed assistance in many activities of her daily life, and
had trouble with her speech and thinking. Prior to her cardiac arrest, Renee had been, by all reports, a precocious child,
a mischievous child, the apple of her father's eye.

The staff came to dread the family's office visits. Renee's parents were thought of as demanding, hostile to the secretaries and unpleasant to other patients in the waiting area. They would sweep in, take up a lot of space, badger the front desk with requests to turn up the lights, to reduce the heat, change the channel on the television, all in tones of barely disguised exasperation. They would yell at the schedulers, refuse to provide documentation for the billing staff, rail loudly about the inadequacy of handicapped parking close to the building.

Once they were in my office, however, Renee's parents would change their demeanor. They were polite to the point of making me uncomfortable; it was hard to get past their bright, shining surfaces. Everything was always "terrific," "best ever," "making superb progress in therapy." These descriptions rarely seemed to correlate with the child I saw in front of me, who had made only minimal advances in any area since she had left the rehabilitation facility to which she had been transferred after her time in our hospital.

I never seemed to be able to get through the parents' veneer; I would offer my thoughts and observations, note how Renee's examination was unchanged, how she had no more words than she'd had three months, six months, nine months ago, but this bad news never seemed to sink in. Renee's parents would just nod, and dismiss my observations with knowing smiles to each other.

One day, Renee's father was on a particularly loud tirade at the front desk, such that I could hear him all the way down the hall through a closed office door. He was so angry that I felt obliged to go down and see what was happening. The front desk secretary was clearly distraught as Renee's father continued to berate her for doing her job poorly, for making "a family with a desperately handicapped child wait like this," suggesting that if "she'd paid attention in school she might be able to type and write faster." The secretary's chin began to quiver, her eyes filled with tears, and the father just became more enraged. "Stop sniveling!" he said through clenched teeth, his face turning purple. "Do your job!"

I walked up to him, and asked him to come down to my office, leaving his wife and daughter in the waiting room. I offered him a seat; he said he'd prefer to stand.

I told him that it was not fair to bully the staff. If he had problems with procedures, or protocol, or any other aspect of his daughter's care, he needed to discuss those things with me. The staff was there to assist me, but was not paid to be abused. His behavior was hurtful to people who were just trying to do their jobs as best they could, and was compromising his daughter's care by alienating the staff. Using his privilege and position to be mean to people because his daughter was ill was not right. If he had not noticed, most of the other families present had children with neurological disorders as well. His daughter's care was important to all of us, but not to the exclusion of others. If he needed to yell, he should yell at me. He needed to be polite with the staff if he wanted to continue under my care.

Renee's father looked at me, stunned. This man, who had been so tightly wound for all these months, began to sniffle, then cry, then sob. I put a hand on his shoulder, and he threw his arms around me, weeping uncontrollably for minutes.

"This is all so hard," he said, over and over, "This is all so hard."

The illness of a child can bring out the best in human nature, and we would all like to think that we would be kind, heroic, and courageous in the context of such an experience. Sometimes this is the case. However, when we see our hopes and dreams for a child dashed beyond recovery, when the life we expected is no longer possible, we often become angry, outraged. Since the universe, or God, or the bacteria that did this is not available to receive our anger in person, those around the sick child often bear the brunt. Minor decisions become invested with huge importance. Staff who are thought of as somewhat peripheral are frequently targets. For Renee's family, it was probably too dangerous to be angry at me; they felt dependent upon my actions and care for their child. The staff, viewed as available targets because of issues of class, race, and gender, bore the brunt of this family's wrath. A mentor once pointed out to me that parents sometimes think with their claws.

Such displaced anger doesn't help the child, the family, or the staff. There are the practical consequences: compromising care by making caregivers so involved in managing the parents' anger that they are less available for other parts of their roles in the child's life, the intrusion such anger represents in the lives of the other families present, the likelihood that observations and complaints from such a difficult family will eventually be disregarded, and hence that something important will eventually be overlooked. All of these things are true.

But I am even more worried about the "soul rot" that such anger represents. To be consumed by such anger means that one's thinking is not clear and that one's emotions hold sway in ways dangerous for everyone. Renee's father was blinded by his anger, and failed to see what his daughter's true state was; he was not preparing her for the life she would in fact be leading. Renee was not going to recover much function, and her parents needed to begin to address what such a life would be like for her and for them. How could they best prepare her for what she would be capable of doing? The father's anger was the chief impediment to moving in that direction.

The father's anger made it difficult for him to discern who would like to help his daughter, who was able to do so, and who was merely trying to avoid them. The father's anger was destructive, in that it blocked his ability to make wise choices in caretakers, therapists, and physicians. In his view, those who aligned with his wrath or enabled it were good; those who did not were bad. This was not a good method for choosing her care team.

Finally, the father's anger made him avoid his own grief and loss, and thus stunted his own growth. As long as he was mad, he didn't have to be sad. But only in acknowledging his and his daughter's losses would he be able to see where his daughter's new possibilities lay.

After a time, Renee's father looked up, found his handkerchief, dried his eyes. "My," he said, "that was embarrassing."

I told him that, like all things said in this office, it would only be shared to the extent that he permitted. More important, I said, was the diagnostic information that his emotional response gave us. He seemed to feel very sad about his daughter, helpless, and angry at her state. Renee's condition, I said, was not likely to change, but their lives could.

I told him I thought the family needed to work with a therapist on dealing with all this, in a way that would be more helpful for their daughter, both now and in the long run. It was too easy, I said, to be in love with the familiar pain and anger he had known since Renee's cardiac arrest. In a way, that anger maintained the illusion that she was still the child she had been before. That was not the case; her illness had changed her, and that change needed to be recognized so that everyone could truly live in this new life.

Change is often convulsive, because it is a recognition of how our lives have been irrevocably altered. If we attempt to deny the changes that illness brings to our lives, our spirits can be possessed of anger and rage that are not useful to our lives. Just as the man in Mark's gospel recognized the face of love in front of him, and thus cleansed his spirit of its uncleanness by abiding in that love, we too can face our own demons and unclean spirits, and remove all that would separate them from the love that is the foundation of the universe.

SIMON'S MOTHER-IN-LAW

The Virtue of Staying Useful

—ℑ—

> Now Simon's mother-in-law was in bed with a fever, and
> they told him about her at once. He came and took her
> by the hand and lifted her up. Then the fever left her,
> and she began to serve them.
>
> Mark 1:30–31

These days, we can read this passage in isolation, and wince a
bit at what it appears to suggest: a woman, an older woman
at that, healed for the sole purpose of waiting on some young
men. It sounds uncomfortably like a way of life we no longer lead—the men folk sitting around and being served, the
women folk working from dawn to dusk and then some. It
makes me think of an episode from my medical school years.

When I was in medical school, we were shipped off for
some "real" medical experience early in our training. The
idea was to acclimate us to the rhythms of life as a physician,
rather than actually letting us do anything. We were far too
early in our training to do anything very useful; I wasn't even
sure how to take a blood pressure measurement. The "shadow-
ing," as it was known, was meant to give us a taste of life as a
practitioner. It was one thing to talk about the pathophysiol-
ogy of diabetes; it was another to see a real live person who
weighed 280 pounds, had a below-the-knee amputation because of gangrene from a wound that healed poorly, was going

blind, and had experienced two heart attacks, all from poorly controlled diabetes.

I was assigned to Dr. B, a venerable practitioner, one of the grand old men of the local medical community a few towns south of the medical school I attended. I was certain he had been present when antibiotics were discovered, and would have put even money on his remembering cupping and leeches. Dr. B moved slowly, at least compared to me, as I was all full of nervous energy in those days. I kept bumping up against him as we made rounds in the community hospital, not being able to judge his starts and stops well.

Dr. B always seemed to have all the time in the world for every patient, yet I came to realize his encounters and visits were often quite short. His ability to be present in every conversation was what created this illusion. Short or long, you always had his whole attention.

I was posted in his office one half day every week, and came to look forward to these times with great pleasure and anticipation. Class work was pretty dreary, and this felt like the only time I was really moving toward my goal.

One day, we stopped in the room of Margaret, a very elderly woman—paper-thin skin, wispy white hair, small bruises where intravenous lines had "blown." Margaret called Dr. B by his first name, something none of the other patients had done. I must have looked surprised.

"Too forward, young man?" Margaret said with a twinkle. "At my age, you can afford to be. Besides, I taught him in high school. I can remember when."

Dr. B smiled, and went on with his examination. He quietly asked how many pillows she needed to sleep comfortably, how much her ankles would swell when she sat up in the afternoon. He told her that he would make some adjustments in her medicines, that this might help. He'd see her tomorrow.

Just before leaving the room, Dr. B looked up and said, "What are you reading these days, Margaret?"

"*Middlemarch.* I commend it to both of you."

He smiled and nodded. "You once told me I should reread that book every few decades, remember?"

"I didn't think you'd listened."

He smiled. "Guess I surprised you," he said.

After leaving Margaret's room, Dr. B and I walked down the hall in silence for a time. Why did he do this? I finally asked. Let medical students shadow him? It must be a bother, slowing him down in his work. And a sort of intrusion, in relationships that had been quite long.

"Why do I do this?" he said in surprise. "You saw in there. Getting old isn't bad. Being useless, that's what's bad. I try to stay useful."

I think of Dr. B and Margaret when I hear the story of Simon's mother-in-law. Work can be a joy, an anchor, a way of connecting to the world around us. Being deprived of anything useful to do is one of the most debilitating conditions we impose on people—prisoners, the poor, the elderly. I like to imagine Simon's mother-in-law as someone who loved her household—the smells of her cooking, the contented noises of hungry people eating a satisfying meal, the banter of table conversation. To be ill was to be torn away from what she loved. The restoration of her health returned her to a place where she could offer people food and sustenance. To be rich means having something to give away, and I imagine Simon's mother-in-law as being returned to a state of generosity by her healing.

THE LEPER

Choosing to Exile or Embrace

—⫴

> A leper came to him begging him, and kneeling he said
> to him, "If you choose, you can make me clean." Moved
> with pity, Jesus stretched out his hand and touched
> him, and said to him, "I do choose. Be made clean!"
> Immediately the leprosy left him, and he was made
> clean. After sternly warning him he sent him away at
> once, saying to him, "See that you say nothing to anyone;
> but go, show yourself to the priest, and offer for your
> cleansing what Moses commanded, as a testimony to
> them." But he went out and began to proclaim it freely,
> and to spread the word, so that Jesus could no longer go
> into a town openly. . . .
>
> Mark 1:40–45

This story begins with choice. The man afflicted by leprosy begins his encounter with Jesus by acknowledging choice: Jesus
can choose to make him clean, free of his leprosy, if Jesus
wishes to do so. We know nothing else about this man save
this: he acknowledges a sort of free will on Jesus' part to heal.
We know nothing in this story about his place in the community, save what we can infer from the fact of his perceived
leprosy. This would have caused him to be outcast, living on
the margins of the margins, rejected and unable to mingle
with others. He would have been excluded from the life of
the community by the fact of his disease.

This much we know, this much would have been known to Jesus and his followers, indeed anyone of that time: the man was a leper and would have be excluded from the world. Lepers were forced to live outside the bounds of society, wandering the roads or hiding in small encampments in waste land. Leprosy was a mark of uncleanness, a sign of divine disfavor. All persons with it were viewed as completely outside the limits of community.

In this story, we know nothing of the rest of this man's life. Did he have a family, a wife and children, before he contracted whatever skin disease was called leprosy at that time? Had he been an honored member of the community, whose fall from a place of high position would have been all the more poignant and horrifying to those who knew him? Or had he scraped by, barely surviving until this disorder thrust him down to an even lower level of his society? We only know he had been a member of the same society as Jesus and his followers, since later comes the admonition to go to a priest to demonstrate his cleansing.

The only thing we know about the leper is that he has been isolated from his community. That would have been all Jesus and his followers knew of him as well, since they were on the road in Galilee. All that Jesus knew—until the man comes up to him, and says a remarkable thing: You, rabbi, somehow have the power to make me clean, to make me whole, to restore me into community, if you so choose. Some sense of the sovereignty that Jesus holds through his Incarnation is clear to this man, whose own incarnation has now taken the form of a disease everyone dreads. These two facts, the man's isolation and his acknowledgment of who Jesus is to him, fill Jesus with compassion. He expresses this compassion by restoring the man into his community.

We can look at this story with post-Enlightenment eyes. We know that a great variety of illnesses were probably called leprosy, incorrectly, in the world of Jesus. We also know that leprosy is not particularly communicable, and therefore did not warrant the extreme quarantine imposed upon its sufferers by the society of Palestine in the time of Jesus. While effective antibiotic treatment for the organism that causes leprosy would not be available until the twentieth century, we know that even without antibiotics the disease is not transmitted from person to person very readily. We can look back, a bit smugly, at a world we view as superstitious and ignorant for treating people in such a way.

I was in medical school when the first cases of the disease we now know as HIV/AIDS began to appear. Certain unusual infections of the gut began to appear in gay men, particularly in cities with a bathhouse culture. These early infections were soon followed by a bewildering array of rare forms of cancer, a breakdown of the immune system, and a variety of strange opportunistic infections. In these early years, HIV/AIDS was an oddity, confined predominantly to the gay male population of certain cities in this country. The disease then began to appear in persons with hemophilia, who had received pooled blood products. Panic spread as the transmissible nature of the disease through various body fluids became evident.

The early days of this plague induced a measure of panic in the medical community. If the disease, eventually found to be caused by an untreatable and novel form of a virus, could be spread through blood, and passed across mucous membranes, through tiny cuts or abrasions, health care personnel were at risk, mortal risk. One of my fellow house officers died of complications of HIV/AIDS, which he had acquired, years earlier, during the resuscitation of a child with hemophilia, a child who also had HIV/AIDS. The threat was real.

Organized medicine reacted in a variety of ways. Large sums were spent on research, first to determine the nature of the infection and its biology, then to develop ways to treat the illness. Hospitals instituted extreme precautions to diminish the spread of the infection to medical personnel. Baskets of protective gowns, face masks with visors to protect the eyes from being splashed, gloves, and Universal Precaution signs became commonplace.

There were other responses that were less noble. Some hospitals began to find ways to turn away patients with HIV/ AIDS, and even those who might be suspected of harboring the virus. Mandatory testing protocols were discussed, and some doctors refused to treat people they deemed "suspicious," or to perform procedures that ran the risk of shedding blood. Quarantine was suggested, and some prominent Christian clergy even said that HIV/AIDS was evidence of God's judgment on homosexuals.

It is worth remembering that the Code of Ethics of the American Medical Association had, in the 1950s, removed any stipulation about treating patients with communicable and infectious diseases. Science had triumphed over infections with the dawn of the antibiotic era, and any such admonition was viewed as quaint, perhaps a bit over the top. When the HIV/ AIDS epidemic began, therefore, secular organized American medicine was caught flat-footed, without a clear set of guidelines for practitioners faced with patients who had an illness that could be transmitted to health care personnel. What were the limits of one's responsibility to patients? In other words, who was included in our community of care, and who was placed outside it? To go back to the debates raging in the medical journals and newspapers of the time is to be reminded that we are not as far from the world of Palestine two thousand years ago as we would like to imagine. It is also worth remembering that the Catholic Hospital Association had never removed language about treating infectious diseases from its Code of Ethics. I like to imagine their memory was longer.

In the story of the leper, Jesus faces a man who is shunned and feared by his neighbors, a man against whom the religious authorities of the Big Tradition in the Temple in Jerusalem would have said all manner of things. Jesus sees a man who is in great need, and a community that is equally in need. He also meets the gaze of someone who looks at him and gets a small inkling of who this Jesus really is. "If you choose . . ." Human authority, human doctors, human healers have not been able to rid this man of his leprosy. The man has some inkling that there is some greater power afoot here.

So he asks for healing, in this particular way. Jesus obliges him, heals him and the community from which he has been severed, in an instant. Jesus then gives two instructions: First, he tells the healed man to go to the priests, the recognized religious authorities, and present yourself according to the rites and rituals of our community. In this instruction, Jesus acknowledges his own continuity with that tradition: Present yourself, he suggests, so that you may be once again incorporated, incarnated, into the life of our community. In this way, you—and the community—will be made whole again.

Jesus gives a second command: Tell no one. The author of Mark tells us that Jesus does this so that he will not be overwhelmed by people seeking cures for their illnesses; the practicality of that notion rings true to our ears. Jesus would soon be inundated by the sick, the halt, and the lame, all seeking cures and healing. His worries were well-founded. But why does he want to avoid this consequence? I think because the essence of his ministry is not the All Palestine League for Healing the Infirm; he has other ideas in mind. Too many people pressing in on him, seeking relief from their illnesses, will not allow him to underline the real import of this ministry: the restoration of community. By sending the healed leper to the priests for certification, he has also sent notice to them: The time has come. The kingdom of God is very near. This man has been healed. While priests and scribes may dither and debate over points of the Law, the people are dying of leprosy, and the community remains fractured.

The HIV/AIDS epidemic can serve to propel us into our worst places—fear, a sense of threat, exclusion, hoarding of vital medicines. It can lead to fractious arguments in our councils, debates about human sexuality and personal morality, authority and power, money and unearned privilege, the sad history of colonialism and post-colonialism. It can also serve to remind us that our brothers and sisters, here and elsewhere, are dying, and that we have within our power something we can do about this. The millions in sub-Saharan Africa, in Asia, in the Caribbean, look at us and say, if you choose, you can help us. You can offer us what you would offer your own brothers and sisters if they had this disease.

If we choose.

THE PARALYTIC

Restored by the Faith of Friends

Then some people came, bringing to him a paralyzed
man, carried by four of them. And when they could not
bring him to Jesus because of the crowd, they removed
the roof above him; and after having dug through it,
they let down the mat on which the paralytic lay. When
Jesus saw their faith, he said to the paralytic, "Son, your
sins are forgiven."

Mark 2:3–5

It is difficult to have a sibling with a significant neurological
disorder. Having a sibling is a difficult proposition in the first
place; so many factors come into play: birth order, talent, competition, the real and perceived slights from other family members. Jacob have I loved. . . .

If we add to all these factors the complicated emotions and
demands placed on the usually developing siblings of a child
with a significant disorder, the result can be a complex mix-
ture of guilt, protectiveness, frustration, embarrassment, pride,
and delight.

My office is also my examining room. The outpatient building in the hospital where I work is a bit crowded, and so we
don't have the luxury of consultation rooms and examining
rooms. The messiness of my office, with piles of papers, books I
am reading, journals half devoured, is there for everyone to see.

One day, a family I had been seeing for some time arrived for their visit, this time with my patient's slightly older sister in tow. Tobias, the patient, was four; his sister Rosa was six and now in "real school," as she said. She had the day off from school that day, and so she had tagged along, since there was no one else at home who could watch her.

We were introduced, and Rosa looked around the room, taking it all in. I offered her some paper, pencils, and books to occupy her while I spoke with her parents and examined her brother. She had just learned to read, she announced proudly. "I can read to my brother now," she said. "I go to real school," she said. "My brother won't be able to go to my school, 'cause he has special needs," she said. "My best friend Alicia, her little brother will be able to go to our school." Then she went back to reading and drawing.

As we finished the visit, I said to the parents, "Do you have any other questions?"

"I do," said Rosa. The parents were amused and slightly embarrassed.

"Yes?" I said.

"Have you readed all these books?" she asked, indicating the two walls of bookshelves that dominate the room.

"At one time or another, yes," I said.

"If *I* readed all these books, *I'd* figure out a way to make my brother all better."

The fame of Jesus has spread so much throughout the countryside that he is now surrounded by huge crowds everywhere he goes. People press in on him from all sides, filling the rooms of the houses where he stays, filling the courtyards, the village squares.

They press in on him, wanting to hear him, to be close to him, to be touched by him. Word is spreading of his ability to perform healing, and people bring the sick, the lame, the blind, the deaf to him for healing.

Four men carry a friend of theirs on a litter. The man is paralyzed; we are not told of the details. Has he been paralyzed from birth? Does he have some form of cerebral palsy? Is he the younger brother or cousin of one of the litter-bearers? Is that why they press in, trying to get this man to Jesus?

Or is he a friend, injured in some accident and left paralyzed? Is his family now bereft, and without someone to earn a living for them in a hard land? Is he a victim of violence, left in this state after a beating? We do not know.

What we do know is this: his friends care for him so much that they will not be put off. Unable to get through the crowd, they climb onto the roof of the building where Jesus is speaking, and begin to dismantle the roof. Jesus must have been standing there, teaching, when he heard the noise above him. Did he figure it out before everyone else? Did he look up in anticipation and smile?

The roof is breached, and the litter lowered. Jesus heals the paralytic man, and we are easily propelled into the rest of the narrative—the argument between Jesus and the scribes, the personification of the lower tier of the collaborating religious authorities in Mark's narrative. We should stop, before contemplating that part of the story, and listen carefully to what Jesus says about the healing.

"When Jesus saw *their* faith . . ." Jesus notes the deep desire of these friends to have their companion made well, whole, included back in the community as a full member, and this is what moves him. When these men will not accept that their friend remain apart, as someone with an illness as significant as this man's would have been in the hard world of that time— that is the moment that sets the mighty act of power in motion. Jesus acknowledges something that has already begun to transpire, through the acts of these four men. It is their headstrong demand that their friend be made part of the community that precipitates his recovery and return to function.

After Rosa, my patient's sister, had made her bold claim about helping her brother, her parents sat and stared at her. They began to say something, then stopped.

"Maybe you should read all those books again," Rosa then added. "Maybe you missed something."

The paralytic's friends and Tobias's sister Rosa will not be put off. When the men in Mark's gospel cannot get through the crowd, they climb the roof with their friend; imagine that for a moment, if you have ever tired to carry someone on a stretcher. Hauling someone up to a rooftop is hard, awkward work. Once there, they burrow through the roof, and lower the man down into the midst of the crowd. They place him at the center of the community, quite literally; once placed there, his rightful position in the community is restored. Their determination is matched by that of Rosa, the little girl who had finally gotten a chance to participate in her brother's visit to the doctor, a doctor who had not yet restored her brother to his rightful place, the place where she wanted him to be: able to participate in the full life of younger brothers. Rosa reminded me of my task.

Restored by the faith of his friends.

THE MAN WITH THE WITHERED HAND
On Cultivating Compassion and Lovingkindness

—ııı⊢

> Again he entered the synagogue, and a man was there
> who had a withered hand. They watched him to see
> whether he would cure him on the sabbath, so that they
> might accuse him. And he said to the man who had the
> withered hand, "Come forward." Then he said to them,
> "Is it lawful to do good or to do harm on the sabbath,
> to save life or to kill?" But they were silent. He looked
> around at them in anger; he was grieved at their hard-
> ness of heart and said to the man, "Stretch out your
> hand." He stretched it out, and his hand was restored.
>
> Mark 3:1–5

I miss a fair number of Sunday worship services over the
course of the year, even in excess of the usual "Episcopalian
summer." When I am on service these days, that is, the attending physician in charge of the team of neurology residents on
call in the hospital, we need to make our rounds every morning. All our patients must be seen at least once a day by all of
us as a team, so we can be sure everything that led to their
being in the hospital is working toward a good outcome. Asking residents to come in very early on Sunday mornings so that
we might be finished in time for me to get to one of the worship services at our parish strikes me as cruel and unusual punishment for the house staff: being on call on weekend days,
being on call and in the hospital for twenty-four hours, is hard

enough, without asking folks to come in extra early just so the attending physician can fulfill some sense of personal religious obligation. Starting rounds after the services would mean keeping the folks on call from the night before in the hospital long after their time to hand over the service had passed; this is even less attractive as a possibility. So, I forgo the worship service. Being on service in the hospital somewhere between twelve and fourteen weeks each year, this mounts up.

I love this story in Mark's gospel. I love this story because of the way it sneaks up on me. Jesus knows from the outset what he is going to do. The man with the withered hand will be healed. The direct beneficiary of this act of power is not really what this story is about for me. I see children with withered hands, that is, loss of muscle tissue from longstanding loss of nerve function; I love to imagine those hands restored. Restored so they could hold their bottles with greater ease, button their shirts with less difficulty, feed themselves with less trouble. Still, as powerful as this image of restoration is, I think it is almost beside the point that Mark is trying to make.

Jesus knows he is being watched, observed by people who have become so centered on the details of the religious laws that they have lost sight of those laws' chief purpose. The Sabbath was meant as a reminder of the deep love of God for humanity. It was meant to give people a small taste, every week, of the kingdom of God: A day when the drives of commerce, of competition, of human greed and striving and self-centeredness, could be put aside for a short time. A day when people could take their rest and restore their right relationships with God and each other.

Instead, Jesus finds himself among people who are so enamored of the fine points of the law that they forget why the law was made in the first place. They have forgotten that the law was meant to help people—in the midst of all their busyness—to have a set of guidelines to keep themselves from falling too far away from the dream of God. These people in the synagogue have hardened their hearts, when the Sabbath was intended to open them.

Jesus asks them a pointed question about the nature of the Sabbath, and they cannot answer. This angers and grieves him, and he then demonstrates the real purpose of the Sabbath by restoring the withered hand. The Sabbath was meant for right relationship, and not as a stumbling block to mercy and forgiveness.

I am not suggesting that we should empty our churches on Sundays, and instead go about some flurry of Good Works. I am also not suggesting that the work I am doing on the Sundays I am not in church is some sort of privileged activity. I am suggesting we need to consider what we do all the time through the optic of the true purpose of the Sabbath, the purpose Jesus underlines here: the cultivation of compassion and lovingkindness.

When I once expressed my discomfort about missing Sunday services for rounds in the hospital, someone told me that what I was doing was probably a good idea in the eyes of the Lord. I thought about this, and for a while tried to practice a different kind of rounds, a more intentional kind of rounds, on Sundays. I tried to use the less hurried pace of the weekend hospital to be more aware of what patients and their families were saying, and not saying. I tried to be more open and generous in my teaching of the residents, and more aware of their struggles. I tried to make myself aware of what each encounter was: something that occurred on holy ground.

To an extent, this worked, but it left me feeling vaguely uncomfortable. Not because this was a bad thing to do on Sundays, but because in point of fact these rounds, these patients, these issues which we faced were no different on Sundays than on any other day of the week. The problem wasn't what I was doing on Sunday; it was what I was doing and how I was being on the other days of the week.

Every day offered the same opportunity, if I wanted to take

it. The Sabbath was not meant to be separate from the rest of life, so much as a reminder for the rest of life. Conducting some sort of more intentional rounds on Sunday was actually no different than going to church on Sunday and then spending the rest of the week unmindful, self-centered, and acquisitive in any job. The point is to be mindful and aware when we are in the presence of God, and that is all the time.

The Sabbath, and the healing of the withered hand on the Sabbath, is meant to remind us how to conduct our lives all the time. Healing is lawful on the Sabbath because healing is an act of compassion, and that is the beating heart of the law. The only purpose of our observance of the law is to make our hearts more open, more aware, more aligned with the dream of God.

THE GERASENE DEMONIAC

Living into the Full Measure of Our Lives

—Ⅲ—

They came to the other side of the sea, to the country of
the Gerasenes. And when he had stepped out of the boat,
immediately a man out of the tombs with an unclean
spirit met him. He lived among the tombs; and no one
could restrain him anymore, even with a chain; for he
had often been restrained with shackles and chains, but
the chains he wrenched apart, and the shackles he broke
in pieces; and no one had the strength to subdue him.
Night and day among the tombs and on the mountains
he was always howling and bruising himself with stones.
When he saw Jesus from a distance, he ran and bowed
down before him; and he shouted at the top of his voice,
"What have you to do with me, Jesus, Son of the Most
High God? I adjure you by God, do not torment me." For
he had said to him, "Come out of the man, you unclean
spirit!" Then Jesus asked him, "What is your name?" He
replied, "My name is Legion; for we are many." He begged
him earnestly not to send them out of the country. Now
on the hillside a great herd of swine was feeding; . . . . And
the unclean spirits came out and entered the swine; and
the herd, numbering about two thousand, rushed down
the steep bank into the sea, and were drowned in the
sea. . . . As he was getting into the boat, the man who had
been possessed by demons begged him that he might be
with him. But Jesus refused, and said to him, "Go home
to your friends, and tell them how much the Lord has
done for you, and what mercy he has shown you."

Mark 5:1 13, 18 19

As a young doctor, I chose my particular residency program for many reasons, a combination of the high-minded and the self-serving. Boston was widely viewed as one of the best places to train in medicine, especially neurology; I was a young man of great ambition. Boston was also the center of the world of behavioral neurology, and Norman Geschwind, one of the true pioneers of the field, was the Chief of Neurology at one of the hospitals in the consortium of institutions where I trained. To be one of his trainees would afford the opportunity for great teaching. He, however, treated only adults. My own path would be one of learning what I could from him, then trying to see how this might apply to children. There were few pediatric behavioral neurologists in those days, and so I looked forward to somehow cobbling together some sort of program that might lead me down that path. I imagined a sort of transitional life, shuttling between the two worlds—Children's Hospital and the Beth Israel Hospital

I loved everything about being at Children's Hospital. The slightly down-at-the-heel faded elegance of the old buildings struck me as very Boston Brahmin. A bit like wearing an old tweed jacket until the sleeves gave out at the elbow, and then putting a patch over the hole. I loved that so many of the names I'd learned in medical school still walked the halls of the hospital. I loved the ethos of the neurology service, the work ethic, and the informality that characterized it.

Most of all, I came to love the associate chief, the man who ran the residency program and served as the chief mentor for all of us. Michael Bresnan was an extraordinary figure, an Irishman, from Cork. He was a superb clinical neurologist, an amazing teacher, the possessor of a limitless supply of jokes and stories, a walking encyclopedia of knowledge about neurology and its history, and a trenchant diagnostician. We all tried to emulate him—his way of thinking through a case, his way of examining a patient, his enthusiasm and energy, his kindness with families. He could think faster on his feet at bedside rounds than anyone I had ever seen. Whenever I had spent all night parsing through a difficult scenario, he always seemed to restate the few salient points after I had rambled on about the history endlessly, generously introducing his remarks with, "So as you say . . ." He would then make a short list of possible causes, eliminate all but one on the basis of things that had been before my eyes the whole time, and come to the answer. He would then invite us to go see the patient to confirm by physical exam what he already knew, confident that he would find the one thing that would reassure us we were on the right track. "Let's go take a little lookie-see, shall we then, boyo?"

He was gentle and tender with families, and I learned from him how to deliver appalling news with truth and compassion. When my excitement about making a diagnosis would start to overcome me, he would quietly remind me that there was a child with that diagnosis, a child who came from a family, and they were all under my care. "We don't use that word lightly with children."

Most of us wanted to be Michael. As I neared the end of my training, I began to rethink my desire to become a behavioral neurologist. I still enjoyed the challenge that such work provided, but there didn't seem to be anyone with whom I could study appropriately. Geschwind had died, suddenly and unexpectedly, during my last year of training; I felt at sixes and sevens. I loved all my rotations with Michael, and thought that perhaps I should just follow his path and become a neuromuscular specialist. I asked for a meeting with him.

"What's on your mind, boyo?"

I said I was going to apply for a fellowship with him, to study neuromuscular disease.

A long pause. "I don't think that would be wise. I'm immensely flattered, but it's not your place. I always thought you would be the behavioral neurology guy for us. I thought of you as our great hope in that field. Those children need better than they're getting, and you could do it, if you had the notion.

That's where you came into this, and I think that's where you should go. So I have to say no. Go back to the behavioral stuff."

I pointed out that Geschwind was dead, and it wasn't clear with whom I could study, with whom it would make any sense to work.

"You took what you could from the best as long as he was with us. Now it's time to move on. We taught you enough child neurology—now it's time to run with it. Those kids can't wait forever. Get on with your life."

The Jesus of Mark is a hard teacher. Sometimes he calls, and sometimes he sends. The message is maddeningly different for everyone, because in the end everyone is met where they are, and sent where they need to be going. A handful of fishermen are called away from their nets, to a life they cannot even imagine. A pious, grateful man, healed of his infirmity, is refused a place on the boat. He stands, watching Jesus and his band disappear across the water, and then turns back toward his own country.

We would all love, at times, to hand over responsibility for our lives, our choices, our gifts, to someone or something else. However, the call of the beloved is not a call to remake our lives along some prescribed line, something we think we ought to be. The call of the beloved is to become more and more who we really are, to live into the full measure of our particular gifts. Simon was called to follow; the Gerasene man was called to stay. They were both faithful to their calls. May we follow their example.

THE WOMAN WITH A HEMORRHAGE AND JAIRUS' DAUGHTER

Touching Power and Faith

Then one of the leaders of the synagogue named Jairus came and, when he saw him, fell at his feet and begged him repeatedly, "My little daughter is at the point of death. Come and lay your hands on her, so that she may be made well, and live." So he went with him.

And a large crowd followed him and pressed in on him. Now there was a woman who had been suffering from hemorrhages for twelve years. She had endured much under many physicians, and had spent all that she had; and she was no better, but rather grew worse. She had heard about Jesus, and came up behind him in the crowd and touched his cloak, for she said, "If I but touch his clothes, I will be made well." Immediately her hemorrhage stopped; and she felt in her body that she was healed of her disease. Immediately aware that power had gone forth from him, Jesus turned about in the crowd and said, "Who touched my clothes?". . . . He looked all around to see who had done it. But the woman, knowing what had happened to her, came in fear and trembling, fell down before him, and told him the whole truth. He said to her, "Daughter, your faith has made you well; go in peace, and be healed of your disease."

While he was still speaking, some people came from the leader's house to say, "Your daughter is dead. Why trouble the teacher any further?" But overhearing what they said, Jesus said to the leader of the synagogue, "Do not fear, only believe.". . . .When he had entered, he said

to them, "Why do you make a commotion and weep?
The child is not dead but sleeping." And they laughed
at him. . . . He took her by the hand and said to her,
"Talitha cum," which means "Little girl, get up!" And
immediately the girl got up and began to walk about. . . .
He strictly ordered them that no one should know this,
and told them to give her something to eat.

Mark 5:22–30, 32–36, 39–43

These two stories, intertwined as they are, both relate encounters where power and faith collide. Jairus, one of the leaders of
the synagogue—not necessarily the kind of man who would
be immediately well-disposed toward a wandering rabbi who
gathers a crowd outside the bounds of the usual religious
structures—throws himself at the feet of Jesus and begs for
his daughter to be healed. In the world of this time, daughters
were of less economic value than sons, but the pain of a parent for an ill child is universal, transcending time and place,
circumstance and customs. The man is desperate, and shows
this. We can assume, by his position, that he could have af-
forded some sort of medical care; we can also infer it was not
successful. He fears for his daughter's life, and comes begging
to Jesus—outside the bounds of the healing arts of the time,
outside the bounds of traditional religious authority.

The woman who ambushes Jesus is also desperate. We
know little of her previous life, save for the medical fact of
her hemorrhage, which will not stop, and that she was of sufficient means that she could exhaust them in the search for
effective treatment. The position of these two people, therefore, is joined. The woman seeks healing for herself, and the
leader of the synagogue for his daughter, but they both seek a
cure that the resources available to them in their places and in
their time have not been able to provide.

The woman intrinsically senses something about the power
of Jesus—that it is physical, that is, part of his Incarnation into

a body. She needs to touch him, or at least his garment, in order to be healed. Jesus likewise heals Jairus' daughter by touch, by contact, by direct physical connection. Power emanates from Jesus without his being fully in control of it. When the woman touches his garment, he senses that power has gone out, but he did not command it to do so. The woman's great yearning—a yearning Jesus recognizes as faith—has led to the unleashing of Jesus' power. Her faith called to his power, and that combination led to a healing. The deep yearning of her soul for wholeness touched the Incarnate power of a God who so loves this world, this woman, that his power rushed out to make her once again in right relation to her body's cycles. The ebb and flow of power between these two people is a microcosm of the yearning of humanity for the holy, and the yearning of the holy to have humanity be well.

Jairus' daughter appears dead, but Jesus maintains that this appearance is a misperception. Death would not have been alien to the people keeping watch over her; they would have seen it often, and were unlikely to make a mistaken diagnosis. No, Jesus says, she is not dead. She is asleep. He touches her, and issues a command—"Talitha cum," "Little girl, arise!" There are three occasions in the gospel of Mark when the author leaves Jesus' words in his native Aramaic and does not simply translate them into the Greek in which the rest of the text is written: This story, the healing of the deaf-mute ("Ephphatha! Be opened!"), and the citation of Psalm 22 by Jesus on the cross ("Eli, eli, lama sambacthani") are the three times the original words are left in place—for emphasis, and to give us a flavor of the man in his native tongue. He commands this little girl to arise, to be awake. His command parallels his command to his followers—be awake, be watchful, the time is coming.

Both the woman with a hemorrhage and Jairus' daughter are healed by contact, by touch. When I was in medical school, we had a course in physical diagnosis during our second year.

It is longstanding tradition in medical education—people have to be taught how to examine a patient, using their hands, their eyes, their ears, in some instances their nose (mercifully, taste has gone by the wayside). Touching patients is a source of great anxiety among most medical students—it was for me. Our society places many restrictions on who we can touch, and how, and where; doctors are allowed to violate those proscriptions in very specified ways and under very specified circumstances. Making the transition from "civilian" to physician has many moments of doing the previously unthinkable; touching patients was one of those.

We practiced on one another, and on paid models. It was awkward and humbling. Most of us had been good at many things before medical school; to be such an abject beginner was not a comfortable position. Imagining that in short order we would be doing this to perfect strangers was terrifying.

In the midst of this class that dealt with mechanics—how to hold a stethoscope, where to place it when listening for signs of pneumonia, how to feel an abdomen for signs of appendicitis, how to elicit reflexes with a small rubber hammer—we had several sessions about touch, and touching. How was clinical touching different from any other kind of touching? What did they both feel like? How could you tell the difference?

Remember, the instructor told us, no matter how incompetent you feel, you enter a patient's room in a position of power. They are sick and vulnerable. They don't know what is happening to them, to their bodies. You have all the power. You are, whether you feel it or not, a medical authority. You know things they do not, and perhaps you know something they fear hearing. You are dressed, and they are partially or completely naked. You are warm, and they are perhaps a bit chilly. You are, I hope, clean, and they may well be dirty. You are fed, and they may well be fasting for some test or examination you have ordered. You are standing up and they are sitting down, or more vulnerable yet, lying down. You may be young enough to be their grandchild. You are about to hear things they haven't told their spouse, and you will examine their bodies in a way no one else does. In all of this, be aware of the power you have, and try to use it well and wisely.

This place you have both entered, the examination room, he went on, is a very privileged one. We might even say sacred. Treat it as such. Communicate your care through your words, of course, but also communicate through your hands and actions. You can convey hope and courage, strength and compassion, by the way you touch someone during your examination. They will remember it all long after you have left the room. If the patient is sorry to see you go, sorry the exam is over, you have succeeded. If you are eager to get it over, they will know this, and you will have failed.

For reasons that sometimes escape me, we are creatures of consciousness who have been given bodies—bodies that will all ultimately fail. For whatever reason, we are incarnate beings. When God, so deliriously in love with these fragile beings that we are, could not convince us of the way we were intended to live with one another, God chose to take on our fallible, incarnate form, and sought us out using the tools such an Incarnation provides. The healing that is offered by Jesus to these two women—one older, one quite young—is a deed of power but is expressed through a very human gesture—touch. Power and longing, faith and capacity, yearning and being, all meet in the healing act of touch.

Today, I will touch a few dozen children in the course of my day. I want to participate in some reflection of that same touch that Jairus' daughter knew, some part of what the woman with a hemorrhage sought. I hope that some small portion of the same love will be communicated to the children I am privileged to touch.

THE ILL OF GENNESARET

Unexpected Grace and Sacramental Work

—╫—

> . . . they came to land at Gennesaret and moored the
> boat. When they got out of the boat, people at once
> recognized him, and rushed about that whole region and
> began to bring the sick on mats to wherever they heard
> he was. And wherever he went, into villages or cities or
> farms, they laid the sick in the marketplaces, and begged
> him they might touch even the fringe of his cloak; and
> all who touched it were healed.
>
> Mark 6:53–56

I am going to recount a love story. Like most love stories,
it doesn't turn out as the principals expect it will, during
the early courtship. Like the best love stories, the relationship turns out to be far deeper than originally anticipated, it
weathers crises that could not have been predicted, and it offers riches that are surprising. And like the best love stories,
the principals are changed by each other.

About fifteen years ago I became interested in why the
parents of children from certain neighborhoods of Boston
were less likely to seek specialty medical care at the teaching hospital where I work than were the parents of children
from the suburbs. Why did children living fifteen minutes
away from the hospital seem to have more trouble accessing
care there than children who lived over an hour away? Given

the inroads that managed care had made in Massachusetts by that time, the answer was not as simple as money. Our faculty practice was compensated roughly the same number of dollars for the care of a child on Medicaid as for a child with most major managed-care plans. There was no financial disincentive to seeing children from the neighborhoods of Boston. I concluded there must be other forces at work.

To understand this situation, I set out to interview the directors of pediatrics at various community health centers in the neighborhoods, the places where most families of modest means sought their regular health care. I started with one particular health center for several reasons, or so I thought. It was close by the hospital, so it might teach me the most about why children were ending up there, rather than at my hospital. I knew the director of a nearby health center slightly. He was one of the grand old men of general pediatrics in this city, whom I had had as my attending teacher briefly during my pediatric internship. He was a wise doctor, a clever and multitalented man, a Brit of great charm and wit, trained at Great Ormond Street Hospital in London, the premiere pediatric teaching hospital in the U.K. If nothing else, my interview with him would be fun. What I did not sense was the breath of God on my neck, the inexorable herding in a direction I did not even know I wanted to go.

The health center is thirty-five years old, one of the oldest in the city. It was born during the high-water mark of the community health movement of the late 1960s and early 1970s, a movement that promoted medicine of the people, by the people, and for the people. It championed meeting the needs of the community in partnership with the community. Medical care for the poor and working class was to be moved out of charity clinics in the hospitals, which always reeked a bit of *noblesse oblige*, and into the community, where it was to be accessible, respectful, and responsive to the needs of the community. Community boards made up of the patients served would run these places, not well-meaning liberals at re-mote teaching institutions whose agendas were certainly mixed, or government functionaries who ran clinics like a medical version of the Department of Motor Vehicles—long lines, ca-pricious rules, ever-changing players. Unlike every other com-munity health center in Boston, this one is still free-standing, still run by its own feisty community board. All other cen-ters have either been acquired by the Health and Hospitals Corporation of the City of Boston, a governmental agency, or are wholly-owned subsidiaries of one of the teaching hospi-tals that dominate the landscape of medical Boston. The great promise of community-based health care was largely compro-mised by its incorporation into the very structures that had made it a necessary alternative. The Health Center is the last person standing. The 1960s lived on in this one small corner of the city.

For whatever reason, I found myself there at the health center, engaged in conversation with the man who would become my part-time boss, cherished colleague, role model, and—probably to his surprise were he to hear this—spiritual director. We talked about my observation regarding access to specialty care, and what the variables might be. How could they be exam-ined? How could they be studied and verified? As he always does, this very busy man acted as if he had all the time in the world for a junior faculty member from an institution whose track record in his own community was at best mixed.

And, as always, he met me coming back the path I thought I was trailblazing. "Well," he said with a gnomic smile I have come to know so very well, "if Mohammed won't come to the mountain, what if the mountain came to Mohammed?"

"I beg your pardon?" I replied, probably speaking more truth than I knew.

"Well, dear boy, neurology has always struck me as a highly portable specialty. A sort of moveable feast. What if you came to the patients? We have some space, you know."

Nearly fifteen years later, I am still waiting to write the paper I set out to research that day. I have, however, seen quite a few patients in an interesting experiment in community-based specialty medical care, more than 800 visits each year. On Fridays, the neurology guy—me—shows up at the health center, and any patients who need to be seen come by. Over the years, other specialties have joined in as well—endocrinology, asthma and allergy, dermatology.

We like to say that we provide the same level of care we provide in our offices at Children's Hospital, but we are wrong. It is better. Better, because we provide care for a hard-pressed community in the context of their lives, and not based on our convenience. Better, because we work in an environment that speaks their language—more than three quarters of our patients prefer to speak Spanish in their homes, and that is the primary language of the health center. Better, because the support staff is all from the community as well. They know the families we serve—which patients are habitually late and which ones need to get to a job or to school on time because a boss or principal is on their case. They know who is homeless and too proud to say it, and who has a child on the honor roll and is too humble to brag about it. Better, because the priorities of the community's health care are set by their representatives on the board, and not by a well-intended director of community benefits at a teaching hospital or a functionary in a government office downtown. The patients I serve at the center are the only poor people I see who have good teeth. Medicaid coverage for dental services is notoriously poor, and so most poor people cannot afford to see a dentist regularly— the out-of-pocket expenses are too high, and their so-called discretionary income is actually used for food, rent, and utilities. When the center had surplus funds from its medical lab, the community decided to underwrite a dental clinic.

Better, because my relationships with patients are more equal and equitable. When I first came to the health center,

I had to pass muster with the community board of directors. Harvard Medical School and the hospital where I usually work have not always been benign presences in the neighborhoods of Boston. It was quite clear from my interview that I was being hired *in spite of* my crimson underwear, not because of it. The board told me that I would have a translator for only the first two weeks of my service there, because that was what they could afford.

Nothing clarifies the mind so much as a lack of alternatives. I took a crash course in Spanish, used the translator for two weeks, and then was on my own. Total immersion on a weekly basis taught me a sort of rough-and-ready Spanish which seems to work. The best part of this experience was the equality it brought to my encounters with patients. I could provide medical consultation to my patients, and they could correct my Spanish, which they have done with grace, humor, and little compunction. Some of my early errors were real howlers, still sources of proverbial amusement with certain families, in much the same way that families retell favorite stories around the Thanksgiving table. The support staff, fully bilingual, became deaf to any English that I spoke. Besides frog-marching my Spanish to a sort of rough competence, this experience bred a camaraderie that abides to this day.

Over the years at the center, I am certain that I have gained infinitely more than I have given back. I have been invited as a tolerated outsider, then a welcome guest, in a community that is habitually made to feel unwelcome in a variety of subtle and devastating ways in our republic. I have come to know the small hopes and high dreams of a stalwart community that most of America likes to pretend doesn't exist. I have been invited to baptisms and funerals, *quincineras* and first communions, graduations and fiestas. I have been a small town doctor in a big city.

I have known Ramon, a young man who was once an honor student despite his attention disorder. During one of his visits,

I wondered to myself if his medication was adjusted correctly to cover his impulsive tendencies over the entire course of the day. I decided that, while the afternoon seemed a bit rugged, his medication was perhaps adequate for his daily activities. After Ramon's visit, the last thing his father said to him as he dropped him off in front of their apartment building before going around back to park the car was "Remember, don't get out on the traffic side." As Ramon ignored his father and climbed out on the street side, a car full of young toughs was being pursued at high speed through the neighborhood by the police. Their car struck him, going perhaps forty miles an hour on the narrow side street. Ramon flew through the air a hundred feet, according to the police report, before landing on the street. On his head. Months later, he was discharged from the rehab hospital that took Medicaid. He has never been quite the same, and, as a result, was forced to leave his exam school and finish high school at a school that could meet his special needs. His father, who worked three jobs to support his family and set aside enough money for Ramon's anticipated college career, has sat quietly with me in a consulting room, and wept for what might have been, as fathers will.

I have known Maria, a young woman who was cajoled and nudged her through high school despite her serious migraine headaches, which her school vice principal assured me were simply malingering, and I have watched Maria become a journalist. When Maria was thirteen, I once asked her what made her headaches worse. She answered, without a trace of self-pity and entirely matter-of-factly, that it was sleeping in the car. Her family had been evicted from their apartment, after her mother found a job which paid more than welfare would allow if they were to continue receiving their housing voucher. The job didn't pay enough, however, to cover the rent, and so they ended up on the street for a time. Graduating near the top of her high school class was a triumph. Watching her go to a local university, graduate, and parlay her degree into a job in journalism, was a delight.

I have known a little boy named José, one of many individuals in his extended family who suffered from attention deficit disorder. Jose's greatest goal in life was to play Pop Warner football. I am not a big fan of contact sports in pre-adolescence, given the risk of injuries to growth plates in the bones, concussions, and the like. However, the Pop Warner program in José's neighborhood is run by a man whom I greatly admire. From the neighborhood, this man, who was once a gang-banger and found his way out of that life through sports, had come back to his community to offer life lessons disguised as scrimmages. Mostly, he offers young men and women a chance for pride, accomplishment, self-discipline, and no excuses. He insists that each touchdown scored be published in the local newspaper, that local businesses post not only the inevitable team picture, but also the academic accomplishments of his players, on their walls. José, whose own father was not present, wanted to play football for this man. Always the smallest in his family, he and I struggled mightily to find a medication for his attention problems, one that would help him stay in class (during one term in second grade, he actually spent more time in detention than in class) and yet not suppress his appetite, so that he could make the qualifying weight and height for the football program. One June, José finally made it—weight and height sufficient so that I could sign his Pop Warner physical. He clutched the paper to his heart, and showed it to everyone in the waiting room. I have seen people less excited about medical school diplomas than he was about his Pop Warner physical.

A few weeks later, I was up in Maine, reading the *Boston Globe* that is forwarded along to me there. I read of a young boy, at Pop Warner try-outs in a city park, who was hit by a bullet accidentally during one of the drive-by shootings that plagued Boston that summer. I was sure I knew that boy, although the paper did not include his name out of respect for the family. I was correct.

José spent a long time in the intensive care unit, and an even longer time recovering from the wounds to his lungs, windpipe, and esophagus. The wounds to his soul are not so easily healed. For a long time, he was afraid to leave his apartment, afraid that "that guy" was still out there and would finish what he had started. José does not believe in coincidence or chance; things have a purpose.

It took a fair amount of browbeating to get the Boston Public Schools to provide in-home tutoring after José's physical wounds had healed. Why can't he come back to school now? the official asked. Because, I said, he is frightened to leave his apartment. He was playing a child's game in a park and he was shot. We lied when we said it was a safe thing to do. It will take him some time to believe us again, when we say it is safe to go to school. But what if every child in such a situation wanted tutoring at home?, the official asked. I paused. Do you mean to say you can imagine a world where this is somehow usual? I said. Where children getting shot while playing is something other than a shock? Doctor, said the official, welcome to our world. Glad you could drop by.

I hung up the phone, opened the door of my office, and looked out on the waiting room full of parents and children— sitting, coughing, reading, sneezing, sleeping, feeding. I was overwhelmed by the immense vulnerability of life, the capriciousness of violence, and the exposure to such injustice that poverty brings. It was not an anonymous thought, a sociological observation, but a fact in the lives of people I knew, cared about, could name.

So this has been my life at the health center. I have been invited to share in the lives of wonderful people, stalwart people, hardscrabble people. I am certain that I could have done something productive academically over this time, could have written articles or perhaps even books, could have attended more meetings in the halls of power, could have taken this time and leveraged it into something that gained me more coin of the realm in which I otherwise reside. Having chosen this work, I instead have become part of a community—even if just peripherally—whose members I love and about whom I care deeply. One day each week, my own private Sabbath, I get to be a bit more like the doctor I hoped I would be when I went to medical school. After a week of petty compromises and machinations, of posing and posturing in the halls of academic power, I get to leave all that behind and come to a community that has taught me much. A community that has taught me about the costs of dreams, and the unmitigated joy of those dreams achieved. A community that wears its heart on its sleeve, and finds physicians that laugh and cry and joyously mangle the language to be a welcome addition. A community that demands much of me morally and spiritually, and settles for small material victories, instead of the reverse. A community that has taught me much about the nature of grace and sanctification. A community that has taught me what solidarity and compassion might look like on a daily basis. A community where my participation is massively unwise and foolish. A community that has given me a taste of the kingdom of God.

Serving this community, even slightly, tepidly, part-time, has been an honor and a privilege beyond any I could have deserved. It is an outward and visible sign of an inward and spiritual grace. My time in this community is sacramental.

THE SYROPHOENICIAN WOMAN'S DAUGHTER

Making Place at the Table

—ᵐ

> . . . a woman whose little daughter had an unclean spirit
> immediately heard about him, and she came and bowed
> down at his feet. Now the woman was a Gentile, of Syro-
> phoenician origin. She begged him to cast the demon
> out of her daughter. He said to her, "Let the children be
> fed first, for it is not fair to take the children's food and
> throw it to the dogs." But she answered him, "Sir, even
> the dogs under the table eat the children's crumbs." The
> he said to her, "For saying that, you may go—the demon
> has left your daughter." So she went home, found the
> child lying on the bed, and the demon gone.
>
> Mark 7:25–30

What are the limits to our community? When we are asked to love our neighbor as ourselves, how far does that commandment extend? Who is my neighbor?

In the story above, Jesus, a rabbi, a Jewish man, is approached by a Gentile woman. The differences of gender and community create a chasm between these two, one that Jesus fairly harshly states. The community of Jewish Galilee is portrayed as a human family, the children of God. The image of the Gentile community is one of dogs—a fairly reviled animal in the world of Jesus and his followers. Yet the woman ignores all these mores and customs, and asks Jesus for healing for her daughter. She asks Jesus to perform the same sort of mighty deed of power for which he has become known throughout the countryside, but to perform it for a Gentile girl, at the behest of her Gentile mother.

Before this story, we have understood Jesus as emerging from a certain matrix, a specific community. His ministry has been understood in the context of that community's history, beliefs, and practices. He has come to fulfill promises he said were made to that community, and restore the right relationship of that community to God, and to restore right relationships among its members.

Today, we too are required to extend ourselves, as Jesus and his followers did when first accosted by this Gentile woman. It is not good enough to talk only to the Jews of Galilee, to offer the gifts of healing and reconciliation to them alone. This woman is beating down the door, and will not be put off.

Medicine reflects the power structures of the society in which it is practiced. In the United States, since the end of the Second World War, medical research has been predominantly funded by the government through the National Institutes of Health. This, in turn, means that Congress, through its funding decisions, sets the direction and tone of research. Those diseases which receive large allocations of money will thus attract larger numbers of researchers. The flow of congressional money tends to direct the flow of new researchers into training. It is not surprising, then, that diseases that afflict middle-aged white men have seen research efforts well-funded over the years, while investigators studying disease processes that afflict children, women, or minorities have often been less well supported.

HIV/AIDS emerged in the late 1970s, primarily as a disease of the gay community. Poorly understood, highly communicable, it was quickly determined to be some sort of viral infection. The machinery of federally supported research began to move, slowly, toward investigation of a novel kind of infection.

For the community afflicted, this funding process was far too slow and far too cautious. Unlike other communities who were prey to illnesses particular to them the gay community refused to be quiet. Adamant, insistent, provocative, often confrontational, they demanded a more vigorous approach to the disease. As a result, in an astonishingly short time, we have moved to an era in which a once uniformly fatal disease has become a chronic and treatable one.

Every day, we offer less than the crumbs under our table to a world that is suffering. HIV/AIDS may be a treatable illness in the developed world, but in Africa, Asia, and the Caribbean it kills huge numbers of people daily. These people are our brothers and sisters. Every day, millions suffer from malaria, and thousands die. These people are our brothers and sisters, and we need to rise up and offer our voices, so that time, talent, and treasure are made available for a global campaign to eradicate malaria. Tuberculosis is once again on the rise, and in resistant and malicious forms. All those who suffer from it are our brothers and sisters.

All these brothers and sisters—are we to tell them that they are not part of our responsibility, not our problem? In the moment of our baptism, we made a promise that we would resist all the forces of darkness, we would struggle against all the forces that corrupt and destroy the creatures of God. We cannot walk away from those promises lightly.

Perhaps we try to wriggle out from these promises by the notion that this is not happening in our community, our little world, our part of the vineyard. I don't see anyone in my parish with tuberculosis, we say. I don't see anyone with malaria. Those things are happening a world away, and are not our concern.

Or perhaps we decide to focus on some other, equally deserving work. Perhaps it is time to rebuild the parish hall, or walk for hunger, or search for a new rector, or support some worthy community initiative. Our time is finite, we say, and we have to do what we do well.

Or perhaps we say that we are too young to make a difference, or too busy raising our family, or too old to make a real contribution.

However we try to evade the question, the Syrophoenician woman sits there waiting for us, with her child possessed by a demon. She does not ask you to neglect your own children, or not build the parish hall, or not walk for hunger, or not be anything other than who you are. She asks you to take whatever you have to spare and offer it to her.

She asked of Jesus something well within his capabilities, and she knew this. He had cast out many demons, and was known to her as one who would undoubtedly have power over whatever demon possessed her child. She also asked him to see with new eyes, to extend the compassion that is at the center of the Law, the promise of God to a world God loves, so that it would include her daughter.

This Gentile woman in Mark is our ultimate ancestor in faith, for few of us are descended from the children of Israel. Our ancestors were, by and large, also Gentiles, not people of the Book and the Law. And every time we pray, or ask anything of God, or give thanks to God, we echo her. She addressed Emmanu-el, God with us, and asked, insisted, that her daughter be within his embrace. If my prayers have been answered, if I taste and see and know the kingdom, it is because she insisted that I had a place there.

When some of her other descendants call to us for help, for mercy, for lovingkindness, what will our answer be? Will her other descendants have a place at our table?

THE DEAF-MUTE

On Being Open(ed)

—⫼

> They brought to him a deaf man who had an impediment
> in his speech; and they begged him to lay his hand on
> him. He took him aside in private, away from the crowd,
> and put his fingers into his ears, and he spat and touched
> his tongue. Then looking up to heaven, he sighed and said
> to him, "Ephphatha," that is,: "Be opened." And immedi-
> ately his ears were opened, his tongue was released, and
> he spoke plainly. Then Jesus ordered them to tell no one;
> but the more he ordered them, the more zealously they
> proclaimed it. They were astounded beyond measure,
> saying, "He has done everything well; he even makes the
> deaf to hear and the mute to speak."
>
> Mark 7:32–37

The choice of words in this story fascinates me. This is one of
the few passages in which the original Aramaic is retained by
the author of Mark. It is a literary choice, a device that is used
for emphasis. We hear Aramaic on Jesus' lips in the healing
of Jairus' daughter and again as Jesus hangs on the cross. In
this passage, we hear just one word, and a command at that:
Be opened.

It is a curious command. Jesus does not cast out a demon
to give the man his capacity for hearing and speech, nor does
he talk about sin as the origin of the man's condition. We hear
no encounter with people scandalized by the healing, and

no discussion of power. Just this command, accompanied by touching the man.

The friends and companions of this deaf-mute bring him to Jesus, and beg Jesus to lay his hands on the man. By now Jesus' reputation is such that they are convinced that his mere touch of their companion will restore him, restore his lost abilities of hearing and speech.

Be opened. But who is being opened, and to what? For what? This idea of openness is what the author of Mark wants us to focus on, since he leaves the word *Ephphatha* in the original Aramaic. This is the idea upon which the story hinges, the fulcrum by which leverage is gained.

Be opened. Opening implies that something was closed. The deaf-mute was certainly closed off, isolated by his deafness and his inability to communicate. In a rural/agrarian, non-literate society, deafness would have cut him off from community in a profound way. Most knowledge in his world was gained through oral discourse. One learned one's occupation, kept one's religious and social obligations, worshiped God and said prayers, obtained daily needs, all through the vehicle of spoken language. This man could not hear what was said to him, and could not be understood by those around him. He was isolated from all the parts of life most central and essential to that time and place.

Be opened. His friends come to Jesus looking for Jesus to lay his hands on the man. Unlike many other petitioners for healing whose stories are told in Mark, this band of people expects no specific outcome from Jesus. They just ask for him to lay his hands on the man. They come to the encounter with a kind of openness that eludes many others who come to Jesus. They are willing to hand their friend over to the power of Jesus, with an implicit trust that whatever happens will be made well, and done well. They echo this later in this story— all is done well, but done well because of their ability to be open to Jesus.

Be opened. The community has opened its ranks to admit this man even before he is healed. The man's companions have sought Jesus out, pushed in upon him, forced their way into Jesus' circle of followers so their friend may be healed. Through this action, through their incorporation of this man into the community, they have been opened.

It is through that opening, that Jesus' mighty deed of power takes place for the man.

Years ago, I consulted for a school system that was embarking upon a fairly radical experiment for the time. They were interested in including a variety of children who would have otherwise been in separate classrooms—children with very significant physical or cognitive challenges that made learning to read quite difficult. Some had been slow to acquire language as toddlers, had never really had the foundational skills in spoken language that serve as one of the underpinnings for reading. Some had sensory impairments, with partial vision or hearing loss. Some were in wheelchairs because of their motor difficulties. In the not very distant past, these children would all have been put into highly specialized classes, with other children who also had significant difficulties.

The director of special education for this school district decided to incorporate such children into a class of more usually developing children, and to assign a "regular education" teacher and a trained special education teacher as a team to lead the class. The idea was rather new then, and quite controversial, especially in a town as conservative as this one was reputed to be.

I sat in on a class, and it was quite remarkable. Children seemed to take their peers with all these various conditions in stride—their banter was like that in any other classroom, their jokes typical of children that age. It did not seem forced or staged. It was just their life as a group.

Later, the director showed me some statistics—reading abilities for students in this combined classroom, with each student's progress charted individually across the months of a school year, compared to a child with similar initial reading ability in a classroom more typically organized, that is, segregated. Page after page showed students excelling in the combined classroom, far outstripping the comparison children in the segregated classroom.

"So," I said, "it seems to work."

The director smiled. "Yes, but not how we expected."

"Why?" I asked. "Didn't you think that the greater social exposure, or the added attention, might lead them to do better? The peer modeling alone was probably quite helpful." It was the basis of the theory supporting this concept of integrated teaching.

"Those aren't the scores of the children with various disorders. They did quite a bit better, too. Those are the scores of the 'normal' children. Being in that class somehow makes them better readers than their peers in regular classrooms."

This effect has been noted elsewhere, and hotly discussed in the literature. Various explanations have been suggested, some reasonable, some far-fetched. I think of this classroom as an icon for our lives. We all do better, in ways we struggle to understand, when we seek to include everyone. There is not one voice, one person, one soul, that does not make us all richer, livelier, more fully who we each are.

Be opened.

THE BLIND MAN

On Seeing More Clearly . . . Day by Day

—ᴴᴴᴴ—

> . . . . Some people brought a blind man to him and
> begged him to touch him. He took the blind man by
> the hand and led him out of the village; and when he
> had put saliva on his eyes and laid his hands on him, he
> asked him, "Can you see anything?" And the man looked
> up and said, "I can see people, but they look like trees,
> walking." Then Jesus laid his hands on his eyes again;
> and he looked intently, and his sight was restored, and
> he saw everything clearly. Then he sent him away to his
> home, saying, "Do not even go into the village."
>
> Mark 8:22–26

There are disorders of visual interpretation by the brain that
most neurologists find fascinating. These are disruptions of
the process of turning bits and pieces of visual data into co-
herent images that a person can understand. The first time we
see a thing that is utterly new, we have trouble processing it
as an image. We need a template to really see anything. Think
of the Native Americans who had never seen a man riding a
horse, an animal unknown to them. The first time they encountered this sight, when European conquerors arrived, they
thought these horse-men were some new kind of human they
had never known before. There are people who, after a stroke
or brain injury, lose the ability to fuse complex visual data into
meaningful composites, who see things as fragmented shards

of information. For example, they can no longer see a telephone sitting on a table next to a bowl of fruit and know this combination of items as a familiar image of their entry hall. This familiar scene has been reduced to chaotic patterns and edges that make no sense. There are people who lose the ability to recognize familiar faces, while still being able to identify people by their voices.

A blind man is brought to Jesus for healing. In his society, in his time, he would have been profoundly disfavored, unable to earn much of a living, unable to participate in the full life of his community. We gather that he does not even live in the village with everyone else, but apart, in some less desirable and hidden place. Still, his friends care enough about him to bring him to Jesus for healing.

In a pattern familiar to us from other deeds of power described in Mark, Jesus spits on the afflicted part and offers a prayer, laying his hands on the man's eyes. The man does not have his vision instantly restored; what he sees at first is deformed and inaccurate—people look like trees walking. My ophthalmologist friends speculate on the exact nature of the man's previous visual impairment, and point out that this partial state suggests a significant astigmatism. That may be accurate, but the diagnosis reminds me a bit of the nineteenth-century attempts to calculate the exact age of the earth based upon the Hebrew Scripture narratives. "Let's see, if Methuselah lived to be . . ." It misses the power of the narrative as metaphor.

Most of the other healing stories we have looked at focus on the re-entry of the afflicted person into community from the perspective of the community. Jesus says that the paralytic is healed because of his friend's faith. Jesus reassures Jairus that the community is wrong in its assessment of his daughter. The healing of the Syrophoenician woman's daughter is about the limits and borders of community. Here, however, we hear about a deed of power work from the perspective of the person who is in the midst of it.

Jesus restores the sight of the blind man, and the man is not quite sure what to do with it. His sight doesn't work quite correctly, or at least as he thinks it ought to work. People look like trees walking. That he can say such a thing suggests that he once had vision, has a memory of what trees and people look like. His vision has been restored, but not quite as he expected.

I think of this man's progress as an image of our life hidden in God. We walk through our lives, often blind to the world around us. Consumed by our own concerns and initiatives, our own devices and desires, we stumble though our days as if blind. One of the expressions many of the mystics use for spiritual awakening is one of vision—sight or insight. Once awakened, we see the world more fully, more wholly, more like God's own vision of the world. We say that we are "enlightened." Yet the vision we obtain is often clouded, or incomplete. Like the man in this story, we see things, but not quite as they are. Our spiritual awakening is one that occurs in steps or stages, not in one great, undifferentiated whoosh.

The story reminds us of this gradual progression. God's deepest desire is to restore us to the state of our natural being, a state of wholeness in which our vision, our hearing—all our senses—are aligned with the dream of God. When we desire that wholeness as well, when we seek that transformation, we are met by God in a way that will help us along. The change, however, is incomplete. Like the blind man in Mark's gospel, we need to return again and acknowledge our limited insight, seek again the healing touch of God's profound compassion for us. Each time we return, we see the world a bit more as God meant for us to see it, as God meant for the world to be. Yet never completely, for our vision always remains somewhat clouded, still providing us with only jumbled images of a half-remembered past.

Most of us have experienced the phenomenon known as *déjà vu*, the profound impression that something new and unfamiliar is somehow something you have seen before, known before. You have never been in this situation, never heard this conversation, yet it is eerily familiar, some memory you didn't know you had until the moment you lived through it. A great variety of neurological theories have tried to explain this phenomenon. Perhaps it is a minute difference in the rate at which information is processed between the two halves of your brain—one hemisphere records an experience milliseconds before the other. It feels familiar to the language-loving left half of your brain because the imagistic right half has already processed it, but had no words for its experience. Or perhaps certain parts of the deep brain that process feeling fire off at random, creating a feeling of familiarity that is not real. Some of our Buddhist brothers and sisters believe that you have experienced a bit of a past incarnation, that some past avatar of yourself has just encountered something it knew, and is breaking through.

All of these might be true, or none of them. I wonder, though, if *déjà vu* actually represents small moments when we awaken, so briefly, to the life we are constantly called to live. Some small moment in which we actually catch sight of the life we are meant to live in the kingdom of God. Some passing moment, some thought, some random bit of visual information, has prompted us to become awake to the life we are always being invited to live. It feels achingly familiar, yet somehow not where we are. For a moment, we are aware how the rest of our life is a form of exile.

Are we physical beings that sometimes have spiritual experiences, or spiritual beings that sometimes have physical experiences? Today, I wonder, throughout all my travels and encounters, did I truly see anything, with the eyes God intends me to have? Or was it all walking trees?

THE EPILEPTIC BOY

Help My Unbelief

―Ⅲ

When they came to the disciples, they saw a great
crowd around them, and some scribes arguing with
them. . . . He asked them, "What are you arguing about
with them?" Someone from the crowd answered him,
"Teacher, I brought you my son; he has a spirit that
makes him unable to speak; and whenever it seizes him,
it dashes him down; and he foams and grinds his teeth
and becomes rigid; and I asked your disciples to cast it
out, but they could not do so." He answered them, "You
faithless generation, ... How much longer must I put
up with you? Bring him to me." And they brought the
boy to him. When the spirit saw him, immediately it
convulsed the boy, and he fell on the ground and rolled
about, foaming at the mouth. Jesus asked the father,
"How long has this been happening to him?" And he
said, "From childhood. It has often cast him into the fire,
and into the water, to destroy him; but if you are able
to do anything, have pity on us and help us." Jesus said
to him, "If you are able!—All things can be done for the
one who believes." Immediately the father of the child
cried out, "I believe; help my unbelief!" When Jesus saw
that a crowd came running together, he rebuked the
unclean spirit, saying to it, "You spirit that keeps this boy
from speaking and hearing, I command you, come out
of him, and never enter him again!" After crying out and
convulsing him terribly, it came out, and the boy was
like a corpse, so that most of them said, "He is dead." But
Jesus took him by the hand and lifted him up, and he

was able to stand. When he had entered the house, his
disciples asked him privately, "Why could we not cast
it out?" He said to them, "This kind can come out only
through prayer."

Mark 9:14–29

This is a story whose truth I know well, on so many levels. It
is an accurate description of the abject terror that a convulsing child brings about in parents; it is a vivid depiction of epileptic seizures. The author of Mark knew of what he wrote. I
once took care of Sara, an infant who had had a few seizures,
and was referred in to the hospital for evaluation. These were
generalized seizures, as we would say, quite like the ones described in this story. The old name for these is *grand mal*, "the
great evil." To paraphrase W. H. Auden, the old masters were
never wrong when it came to suffering.

Sara's seizures stopped with the administration of some
medication given through an intravenous line we started. She
settled down, breathing more comfortably and looking at peace.
Her parents, a young couple, looked relieved that this bout
was over, but clearly frightened.

"How long has this been going on?" I asked.

"Off and on, since late last night," Sara's parents said. They
had taken her to the local hospital after the second seizure.
The doctor on duty had experienced trouble getting an intravenous line into a small, convulsing infant. She had given the
baby some medicine by a shot into the muscle, and arranged
for transfer to our hospital. En route, the infant had experienced two more seizures; the paramedics had given medication by suppository, and the seizures had again stopped. She
arrived in our emergency department, and had started seizing
again. More medicine, this time by the successfully placed IV
line, had stopped them.

As we sat talking, going over the pregnancy, the family's

medical history, the child's illnesses to date, Sara began to convulse again. The seizure lasted five minutes; more medicine was needed to stop it. The sort of anti-seizure medications used in such acute situations often slow down the brain's commands to the lungs to breathe; Sara's breaths were a bit shallow and sounded husky. The decision was made to protect her airway, by placing a breathing tube down her throat. She would have to go to the intensive care unit.

The family, panic again rising in their voices and fear quite palpable in the room, looked at me and said, "She's going to be okay, isn't she?"

I believe; help thou my unbelief.

"She'll be safe in the ICU; we can give her as much medicine as she needs to control these seizures, now that she has the breathing tube in." I said.

I believe; help thou my unbelief.

The day wore into night, and Sara's seizures kept coming. One medication was given to its maximum dosage; a second was added. It, too, was given to its maximum, and still the seizures kept coming. In the midst of all this, we looked for signs of what might be causing such intractable seizures. Sara had a spinal tap; there was no infection. She had blood tests; none suggested any inborn error of metabolism that would create such recalcitrant epilepsy. An EEG of her brain function showed a very disorganized background resting state to her brain's electrical activity, and bursts of ugly-looking seizure activity.

We struggled on through the night, trying to bring Sara's seizures under control. More medicines were started; each seemed to get things to slow down, only to have the seizures return. Trips by the parents to and from Sara's bedside, trips by the medical team to and from the waiting area. Alternating hope, as things looked good for a few minutes or perhaps an hour, only to be followed by more convulsions.

We finally decided that the only thing left to do was to place Sara in a coma—the thought being that if we put the brain completely to sleep for a while, when we awakened it the seizures might have stopped. I explained this to the family.

"You're going to reboot her brain?" the father asked, incredulous. The mother looked terrified at the idea and horrified that her husband had expressed it like that.

"I hadn't thought of it that way, but yes."

We put Sara into a coma, and then waited for a day, two days. After a time, we decided to awaken her. It took almost two more days before all the medicine cleared her body. Sara began to react—first by withdrawing from an unpleasant stimulus, then by trying to push it away. She finally opened her eyes, and looked at her mother. She smiled. Her mother and father, at her bedside, broke down and wept.

Sara was transferred to the neurology ward a day or so later. We needed some time to stabilize her medications, to find a combination that would keep her seizures under control and still allow her to be awake, to sit up, to eat, to interact with her parents. I felt like we were walking around on tiptoes, waiting for the seizures to start again. They didn't. Sara was able to go home a week later.

We set up an appointment to see me in a few weeks, and I gave Sara's parents my card with my pager number on it. If anything happens, I said, give me a call. Anytime, night or day. Neither they nor I said what "anything" was; it felt as if saying the word might make it happen.

A week later, I was leaving the hospital after a long day, when my pager went off. I cursed under my breath, and found a phone. Sounding exasperated, I'm sure, I identified myself as the page operator made the connection. "Urion. Neurology." I was certain it was some family who had forgotten until the last minute to call for a refill on their child's medication. With all the office staff safely home, it would be up to me to find the chart, verify the dose, call the pharmacy. I was getting ready to deliver the lecture on timeliness and Making Sure to Plan Ahead.

"Hello?" Sara's mother identified herself, with a catch in her voice. "She's doing it again. It started this afternoon. Short little ones, at first. I didn't want to think that's what they were. But they kept getting longer, and she cried before each one. And this one, this one doesn't seem to be stopping. . . ." Her voice trailed off. I heard her crying.

We arranged for an ambulance, and got Sara to the hospital. We went through another several rounds of medication, another intubation, another decision to place her in a coma.

Once again, the coma stopped things for a while. Sara again awakened, and was again able to go home. For a time.

Then one day Sara's parents came into my office, holding their baby daughter. We had achieved some measure of control over Sara's seizures, but she slept nearly all the time.

"This isn't a life," Sara's father said. "It's just not right, her being like this all the time."

I agreed it was an awful bargain—awake and seizing, or sedated and under control.

"We've thought about it. We want to back off on the medications. Have our baby back, even for a little bit. Then if she seizes again—" He winced. "Actually, when she seizes again, could we just make her comfortable or something? I mean, not all that other stuff? Just make her comfortable? Could you do that?"

I said we could, yes.

"Not everyone, or anyone, could *you* do that? I mean, we started with you, we want to finish with you."

Yes, I said, I could do that.

"Okay. Then how do we start?"

We came up with a schedule to reduce Sara's medications. The family went home, and put the plan into action. We spoke every day, and soon the seizures began again.

"Do you want to be here, or at home?" I asked them over the phone.

"This is a little hard, all alone. If we came in, would people stay with the plan we came up with?"

Yes, I said, I would admit her to my service, and I would make sure this was so.

They came in, and Sara seized more and more. We gave her

some Valium to relax her muscles a bit, and some morphine for pain. Her seizures became longer, and her breathing more troubled through each one. Finally, during one long seizure, Sara became breathless, and then turned blue. In a short while, her heart stopped.

I know the story of the epileptic told in Mark's gospel. I know the pain and the worry of the father, and his anguish, caught between belief and unbelief. I know his horror at watching his child convulse, and throw himself in the fire and the water. I know the helplessness of the disciples, unable to find the remedy for the boy's convulsions. I know what it is like to look for answers, and debate with the scribes, and consult the texts, and find nothing. I know what it is like to be unable to pray.

I believe, only help thou my unbelief.

BLIND BARTIMAEUS

Seeing Others Truly

—ᛜ

. . . . As he and his disciples and a large crowd were leaving Jericho, Bartimaeus son of Timaeus, a blind beggar was
sitting by the roadside. When he heard that it was Jesus
of Nazareth, he began to shout out and say, "Jesus, Son
of David, have mercy on me!" Many sternly ordered him
to be quiet, but he cried out even more loudly, "Son of
David, have mercy on me!" Jesus stood still and said, "Call
him here." And they called the blind man, saying to him,
"Take heart; get up, he is calling you." So throwing off his
cloak, he sprang up and came to Jesus. Then Jesus said to
him, "What do you want me to do for you?" The blind
man said to him, "My teacher, let me see again." Jesus said
to him, "Go; your faith has made you well." Immediately
he regained his sight and followed him on the way.

Mark 10:46–52

The arc of the healing stories ends here, the last to appear in
Mark's narrative. From here, the story will grow darker, slowly
at first, but inexorably, like clouds on the horizon, a squall line
that comes closer and closer. The entry into Jerusalem, first in
triumph, then to execution. But before all that, this is the last
mighty deed of power that Mark recounts.

It is emblematic of what these stories have been trying to
tell us. Bartimaeus, the blind beggar, the one we see every day
by the roadside, the one we ignore, the one we don't talk to,

demands to see Jesus. He's a bit mad, really, screaming and caterwauling like that. He is strident, and pleading, and quite inconvenient: "Jesus, Son of David, have mercy on me!" It is a version of the Jesus prayer; we hear it here for the first time.

The well-mannered disciples, the handlers, the entourage, they want this embarrassing man to go away. Be quiet, the rabbi is talking about important things. Bartimaeus will not be silenced.

When I rotated through adult neurology, the Chief of Neurology at one of the hospitals was a figure we residents held in a combination of dread and awe. He was austere in manner, profound in his knowledge of neurology and its history, dismissive of people who tried to bluff their way through his rounds, and fiercely devoted to his patients in a patrician fashion.

I was once assigned to examine an elderly African American woman. She was said to be "slowing down." I went in to see her, and trotted out my best bag of mental status examination tricks. Count backwards by seven from 100. Not possible. By fives. Equally impossible.

Who is the President? She had no idea. The last several Presidents? Weren't none worth nothin' since Franklin Delano Roosevelt. A sentiment my family shared, but not the answer I was seeking.

This process racketed along for an hour, and in the end I came to the conclusion she was quite demented. Rather advanced Alzheimer's, I thought. I looked for signs of other forms of dementia on her examination, and found none. Her condition seemed perfectly clear to me. For once, I thought, I'll be ready for rounds.

I presented the case to the chief. I recounted her history, as I knew it—She was visiting a son in Boston, who became concerned regarding her "slowing down" and brought her in. I told of her examination, in lurid detail. I came to my conclusion—Alzheimer's disease, reasonably advanced.

Well, said the chief, shall we see her? For once, I wasn't afraid. I was sure there was little he would find that wouldn't be included as part of what I had already found. More elegantly demonstrated by the chief, perhaps, but I doubted I had left anything out.

"Hello, ma'am. Dr. Urion tells me you're up here visiting your son."

"Yes, sir. Fine boy he is."

"I'm certain of that. What does he do?"

"Drives a bus. Local bus. Goes right by B.U. You know, that's where Dr. King became a doctor."

The chief smiled at her, sweetly, and at me, somewhat less sweetly.

"Yes, that's quite true. He said he liked his time in Boston, I believe. Only it was cold."

"Well, he got that right." She laughed, and the chief joined in.

"Where did you come from, to visit your son?"

"Mississippi, sir."

"And what do you do there?"

"Not much anymore, since the rheumatism got me. Used to farm, though."

"Really? Sharecropping?"

"Yes, sir. Chopped cotton. And had a little garden."

"How much cotton could you chop in a day?"

They proceeded to engage in a detailed discussion of the economics of cotton sharecropping, the relative merits of various strains of tomatoes, the correct preparation of okra, and which hens were the best layers. After an hour's barefoot romp through the delta, the chief finally said his good-byes.

"We'll not trouble you anymore today, ma'am. Thank you for your patience."

Once out of the room, the chief looked at me with his hooded eyes.

"Dr. Urion, please never confuse failure to go to school with dementia, or illiteracy with real ignorance. Your exam failed because you didn't bother to find out who was sitting in front of you. Context is quite important. Please don't forget." He turned, and walked away.

Bartimaeus insists on being seen and heard by Jesus, for who he is and what he is. Jesus makes no presumptions, but instead asks Bartimaeus what he desires. Bartimaeus answers, and Jesus restores him.

Although he is blind, Bartimaeus actually sees quite well. He knows who Jesus is, calls him by one of his names, knows that he is a source of mercy and healing. He calls to Jesus in prayer—have mercy on me. Bartimaeus calls as he is, in the midst of his outcast state, without pretense or disguise. Jesus' followers cannot see this wretched man as one of them, one of the faithful, one of the chosen. They see only a blind beggar, howling and wailing at the side of the road. An embarrassment, not part of the important work they feel they are about.

Bartimaeus will not be silenced, and Jesus hears his cry. He sends for him, to make his point that this man, from the entire crowd pressing in, is being especially called out. Jesus then asks him what he wants, making no assumptions, meeting honesty with honesty.

And given his straightforward answer—let me see again; let me see the kingdom again—Jesus heals him, and the first thing those healed eyes would have gazed upon was the face of Jesus.

When any of us sees another person as he or she truly is, sees that person with eyes of love and compassion, what we look at is the face of Jesus. The moment I am ready to join Bartimaeus and ask to see again, that will be the moment that I see the face of Jesus. If my prayer is answered, the face of Jesus is all that I will see in the face of anyone I meet.

Having given this last example, this last mighty act, Jesus is now ready for the long walk that will lead first to the place of the skull, and then back again to Galilee.

3

Community Restored

—ᚊᚊ—

YOU ARE NOT FAR FROM
THE KINGDOM

—Ⅲ

One of the scribes came near and heard them disput-
ing with one another, and seeing that he answered them
well, he asked him, "Which commandment is the first
of all?" Jesus answered, "The first is, 'Hear, O Israel: the
Lord our God, the Lord is one; you shall love the Lord
your God with all your heart, and with all your soul,
and with all your mind, and with all your strength.' The
second is this, 'You shall love your neighbor as yourself.'
There is no other commandment greater than these."
Then the scribe said to him, "You are right, Teacher; you
have truly said that 'he is one; and besides him there is
no other'; and 'to love him with all the heart, and with
all the understanding, and with all the strength,' and
'to love one's neighbor as oneself,'—this is much more
important than all whole burnt offerings and sacrifices."
When Jesus saw that he answered wisely, he said to him,
"You are not far from the kingdom of God."

Mark 12:28–34

One of my patients is a child with cerebral palsy. Jeffrey was
born very prematurely, and had most all of the complications
one could have from prematurity, being born after twenty-
seven weeks gestation. He needed a breathing tube and artificial ventilation for a long period of time, and his lungs suffered
for this: he has a form of asthma which still plagues him. He
received significant amounts of oxygen through his breathing

tube, and he has poor vision, in part as a consequence of this. He lost part of his intestines, a result of an infection which killed part of them off and required several surgeries while he was still a newborn.

Jeffrey has a seizure disorder, and requires several anti-epileptic drugs to keep these seizures under a semblance of control. He has "breakthrough" seizures when he gets a cold or an infection, even if his family is vigilant and starts medicines against fever at the earliest possible sign. He cannot walk any real distance yet, at age five, although he has recently learned to stand without holding onto something. He wears braces on his legs, and needs physical therapy twice daily. He was late to talk, and still has significant language troubles. His words are often hard to understand, being slurred and with various sounds substituting for others. Cognitive testing suggests that his overall intellectual functioning is at the very low end of the normal range, and may well prove to be in the mentally re-tarded range as tests become more accurate as he grows older.

Jeffrey's family adores him. They take superb care of his needs, day in and day out. They take him to his myriad appointments with all the doctors and therapists that constitute his team. They advocate for him in the school system, trying to balance the needs that require separate instruction from his peers, with his and their desire for him to be with more usually developing children as much as possible. Yet Jeffrey's life is not all work and therapy. He and his family do things all families do. He and his father go fishing; their boat has special adaptations so he can get in and out more easily, and sit well-supported while on board. His mother is teaching him to paint with specially adapted equipment.

When Jeffrey's parents began their life together, this cannot be what they expected. This could not have been their dream when they became pregnant. Like most couples, they said, they thought about names for the baby, what color to paint the room. Would he grow up to be a doctor, or a lawyer, or a sports star? Would he have his father's dimples, or his mother's easy laugh? Would he hit the winning home run in Little League, or score the winning goal in soccer? Will he be rowdy, rough and ready, or a quieter, more thoughtful child? They moved to a town with a strong school system, and good sports programs— they wanted the best for their unborn child. Whatever they imagined, the life they now lead was not part of their dreams and worries, hopes and fears, during pregnancy.

All this came crashing down when Jeffrey's mother went into labor at twenty-seven weeks, and the labor could not be stopped. Jeffrey arrived, and his parents were plunged into the brave new world of the intensive-care nursery. Words and concepts and worries they had not even imagined now became commonplace. A strange land of incubators, intravenous lines, respirators, head ultrasounds, brain hemorrhages, destructive gut infections, tired residents and fellows who seemed far too young to understand what they were trying to tell the family, far too young to be doing what they did. It seemed, Jeffrey's father once said, to be a children's crusade.

The couple survived, and so did Jeffrey. He came out of the intensive care nursery, "graduated" to the regular nursery, and then went home. Later, the family weathered further hospitalizations for pneumonia, operations on his legs, removal of scar tissue that blocked his gut. They learned new skills, and new worries.

The family came into my practice when Jeffrey was three. Children leave the newborn follow-up program in our hospital at that age; they pass on to some other member of the department. We weathered the first few visits together, finding out who we were for each other. All physicians have a style, a rhythm, a way of working; mine was different from their previous neurologist's, and we felt for a while like we were dancing the wrong steps to the wrong music. With time, we got better at it. I learned to read their voices, to know when a seemingly innocent question covered great anxiety, and when it was merely gentle curiosity about something. They learned my peculiar wish that they page me directly when we needed to talk, my somewhat obsessive need to remove the filter of support staff or nurses when we were talking about their child's health. "We hate to bother you," they said. "Really, no bother," I insisted. "I'm in so many different places, I wouldn't know where to tell you to leave a message." All frightfully polite, these early misunderstandings.

I came to admire Jeffrey's parents greatly. I try to remember, before every visit with every patient, that each person that comes through the door is all that I may see of God that day. With this family, it was somehow easier to remember. They were kind and gentle with their son while still managing to treat him much like any other five year old when he became willful or whiny. They seemed to have achieved a balance between mindful care of a child with complicated needs and the emotional space of a family with a five-year-old boy.

We were talking one day about an upcoming meeting with school staff regarding plans for Jeffrey's placement in first grade. He was making the transition from the special-needs setting in which he had been since age three to what he called "real school." They were insistent that he be in a regular class, perhaps going to get physical therapy when the other children had some free time, and getting speech therapy at some equally unobtrusive time. Otherwise, they wanted him with his peers. He was going to be a member of the class, not somebody who came in every now and then for his "integration time" with peers. They did not want him in either the substantially separate classroom in another school in the district, or in the highly specialized school setting for children with significant physical handicaps in a collaborative school run by several local school districts. They had no reason to believe, they said, that he couldn't prosper in a regular classroom with some adaptations for his physical needs. They negotiated these needs every day, many activities at home being more challenging—getting in and out of the tub, getting in and out of the car, encouraging their son's independence while attending to his needs for assistance. They had balanced these needs for a long time, and had done, I thought, quite well. They were asking far less of the school.

"The school keeps couching this as an issue of safety, but really, his asthma is not that bad, and his seizures have been pretty well-controlled now for a while. I think they're just hiding behind that," said the father.

"We just want him to be there, and see how he does. It will be a struggle, I'm sure. But he's here. He deserves a place in the school. This is our town, and that is his school. We're not asking for some out-placement, some expensive program at some fancy place, like some of the other families in the special-ed parents group. You'd think the administration would be happy," said the mother.

"I think they're just uncomfortable with children who have physical needs. I think they're more uncomfortable than his peers are. He gets invited to birthday parties all the time. He's great company," added the father.

We talked about strategies to address the school's professed worries, and what other attitudes might be hiding behind that. We talked about the regulations, state and federal, and what they might mean for Jeffrey. We agreed to talk on the phone after their meeting at the school. I would prepare a letter, just outlining Jeffrey's likely needs and issues—which, if anything, were less significant at age six than they had been when he first entered the school at age three.

We finished our conversation, and then the family began to organize to leave. Bags and wheelchair, walker and braces. "We don't travel light," said Jeffrey's mother, laughing.

"Well, thanks, as always," said the father.

"No, thank you," I said. " You are a remarkable family, and it's a real pleasure to work with you. This is a hard road, and you travel it with real grace. I always feel lucky to work with you."

"Well, thanks, but the praise is not really deserved. I mean, I'm the lucky one," the father said. "Having Jeffrey was the best thing that ever happened to me. I mean, really, most people find that surprising when I say it, but I mean it. Before he was born, I was just hell-bent on everything being just right. Had to be perfect. The best car, the best job, the best house, the best everything. And I worked like a maniac. To provide more of that best. Worked all the time. Really competitive. More billable hours than any other first-year associate. Made partner before anyone else. Ruthless, competitive. Right for the jugular. Bang! I was on my way to becoming a real asshole."

"Yep, he was," laughed his wife. "No doubt about that."

"You're not supposed to agree that quickly," he laughed in turn. "Anyway, then Jeffrey was born. And everything changed. Everything I thought was important, all of a sudden wasn't important. At all. I mean, it was great, getting good care, being able to afford what we needed, all that. Don't get me wrong. But at the end of the day, my son needed me. Who I was, and who I could be. And my wife, she needed me. So I had to change. I mean, I had to live what my life had become. Like, this is your life, now, buddy, you better show up. There is no "complaints and returns" desk in this universe. You better deal with what's in front of you."

How do we understand the nature of healing? What do we mean when we say that someone we love has been healed, or that we have been healed? I understand some of the complexities of my work through models, none of which is perfect, each of which grasps some part of the truth. In different settings, certain models work better than others. For example, sometimes it is useful to describe an epileptic seizure as being like static in the brain, comparing the ongoing thoughts to a radio program. Sometimes it is more useful to describe a seizure as a storm, passing over an always changing ocean that becomes tumultuous in such circumstances. I would like to consider the different ways we think about healing.

What does it mean to love God with all your heart, and all your soul, and all your mind, and all your strength? What does it mean to love your neighbor as yourself? These questions are at the core of our thinking about how to live. They are the core of Christian ethics. William May, in his wonderful book *The Physician's Covenant*, speaks of using icons as a way of thinking about ethics. Words can fail, and often separate us through misunderstanding or misperception. First principles can become rigid and codified. The Law can be cruel and harsh. May suggests that we think instead of images, icons, as we consider what we are to do in a given arena.

The concept of healing can be considered in several different ways. Healing can be a cure, the removal of some cause of illness or disease. Healing can mean remission; some chronic condition can cease to be bothersome for a time: we know we live with it, but for now it does not trouble us. Healing can be reconciliation: two conflicting aspects of our lives or conflicting people in our lives can be brought together across the chasms that separate them. Healing can be acceptance: This is our life, this is our path, and we will walk it with all the grace we can, as long as we can. I would like to consider the implications of these different images of healing.

Cure. Every person I have ever met—every patient, every parent, every physician, every therapist, every nurse, everyone I know—hopes for a cure for the illness or disorder they face. We all have some sense of what it means to be whole, unafflicted, and healthy. Much of the work of people in my department is geared toward prevention of the sorts of problems with which my patient Jeffrey was born, and much other work centers around turning around the damage that parts of the nervous system experienced during Jeffrey's first weeks of life. As a department, as a discipline, as a society, we strive toward curing a variety of medical illnesses. As a community, we can understand this desire for a cure in the context of our baptismal vows: "Do you renounce the evil powers of this world which corrupt and destroy the creatures of God?" Many illnesses and disorders can be understood as working against the well-being, the order of the universe, God's dream for humanity. It is difficult for me to look at infants who struggle against infections like the ones Jeffrey did in his early days, or at HIV/AIDS orphans, or at children who have been beaten and injured by people who were meant to care for them, and not consider to afflictions to be the work of some power which destroys and corrupts what was intended to be lovely.

It would be wrong, however, to twist this idea so that we think of those who have such illnesses as in some way corrupted, less than whole, incomplete members of the kingdom. Illness is not a mark of divine disfavor. We may smile when we read gospel stories in which epilepsy, an illness whose biology we know and understand, is described as demonic possession, the work of "unclean spirits." We can smile at this, dismiss it as a primitive belief and those who held it as deeply superstitious. Yet if we scratch our own supposedly sophisticated thinking, we find that this primitive idea still lurks not very far below the surface.

The stigma that children with HIV/AIDS have faced recently in this country is not all due to worries about contagion; few body fluids are cross-inoculated in the classrooms of this country. I think our discomfort with these children stems from ancient notions of being "unclean," of somehow being not fully human or not a member of the community as a result of this disease. We see its means of transmission as some kind of proof that its stigma is divinely ordered. Some clergy have called HIV/AIDS God's retribution on groups of people who have, in their view, sinned; religious communities have placed judgment before compassion. Children born with HIV/AIDS have found that the ancient idea of the sins of the parents being visited upon their children persist. There is little medical justification for the behavior of certain school districts in the early days of this plague, which isolated and shunned children with the retrovirus. We are not as advanced as we might think.

Children with cerebral palsy can also find themselves stigmatized. Because a cure for their difficulties is not available at present, their problems persist in public. Our reaction to such children who cannot be cured of their spasticity, whose seizures will not go away, is a sort of litmus test for our relations with other children whose problems are less severe. If children whose difficulties cannot be cured make us so uncomfortable that we seek to segregate them from the rest of the community, then that tells us that everyone's place in the community is determined by their achievements and abilities. That is, if Jeffrey is not fully welcome in a public school because we cannot make his manifest physical challenges go away, then it is not a far step to say that the child with the recalcitrant reading disorder is also not welcome, that the child who struggles with climbing the rope in gym is not fully a member of the community.

If some communal notion of wholeness or health becomes the definition of who can be a member of the community, then we will struggle forever with the definition of how whole one must be in order to be included. Must one read well, write well, play music well, excel at sports, be thin, be affluent, be of one race or another, in order to be included? This slippery slope is a bad one, and the twentieth century taught us where it leads. The Nazis were first legitimized by academic physicians, pediatric neurologists in many instances, who argued that the community would be improved by the removal of diseased members, just as a patient would be improved by the removal of a gangrenous limb. Certain people became identified with certain aspects of their lives, and those lives were equated with a disease on the body politic that required radical surgery. Once we begin to use the ability of some difference to be removed, to be "cured," as the threshold that must be crossed before one can enter into full participation and membership in a community, we have then said that membership in community is conditional. And if such membership is conditional, then where and how and by whom the lines are drawn can begin to be a rather ugly process.

This kind of conditional acceptance also changes the concept of a cure from a marvelous gift, a wonderful event that represents a grace in an individual life, to a barrier that must be breached. If cure is not a free attribute available to all by their nature as humans, but rather something that is a delimiting condition, a price of admission, then cure becomes a commodity. It can be given a material value, a cost, and we can discuss who can afford it, and who cannot. We have decided that human enterprise and commerce have become the determining factors in the striving toward such cure. This means, in turn, that resources and attention will be turned toward the needs and interests, the hopes and desires, of those who already hold the levers of power. It is no idle turn of phrase when medical practitioners speak of "orphan diseases" and "orphan drugs," illnesses that afflict people so marginalized that the medical system does not expend time or energy on seeking cures for them, treatments for illnesses so rare that it does not make economic sense for pharmaceutical companies to expend time and money producing them. If cure is solely organized so that people deemed defective, less than whole, or incomplete can be made complete in order to enter society, then cure will be a process that recapitulates many of the inequalities and prejudices that haunt our world. Cure will be as limited and imperfect as the human heart.

Remission. Some illnesses and disorders can be pushed back, so that a semblance of more normal function, of a more typical life, is returned to the person suffering from them. We often think of remission in relation to cancer or a chronic infectious disease. The term has ominous overtones: It implies that whatever victory has been experienced over the disease process will be short-lived. It implies that the disease has fallen back, but is regrouping, lying in wait to attack again when we least expect it. My mother had breast cancer, which was treated so that she had a long, and wonderful, period of remission. We all lived that time sensing something of a borrowed nature to it. When her cancer recurred, it was not a surprise. In some part of our hearts, we had been expecting its return all along.

In some sense, my patient Jeffrey experiences remission of parts of his illness for long periods of time. As time has passed, we have gotten better and better at controlling his seizures. Part of this success is due to new and better medications having become available over time. Part of it is due to my getting to understand Jeffrey's seizures better—their triggers and their patterns. This learning process reminds me a bit of my grandfather's sense of fishing. Given a place and sufficient time, he gradually came to know when and where the fish would likely be. My experiences of watching him glean that knowledge in a new fishing spot recur to me as I come to understand the seizure patterns of a given child. It is a process that requires the incorporation of information from various realms and senses, coupled with careful and attentive listening and watching. Yet for Jeffrey, we know that sooner or later, despite all our efforts and care, his seizures will return. Their recurrence is always a disappointment; sometimes it is a danger.

How, then, do we live with remission? What does it tell us about ourselves, and about the place of the person experiencing such a remission in our community? Remission of Jeffrey's seizures certainly makes his time in the community of his school easier. The longer the period of remission, the more comfortable his teachers and parents feel, the easier it is for the administrators to feel comfortable in their responsibility. It makes it easier for him to learn—he doesn't miss time from school recovering from bouts of seizures. Remission has many practical advantages.

The uncertainty that hovers over remission can be a positive or a negative force; depending on how the community handles it. If we hover and fret and spend a lot of time and energy waiting for the inevitable relapse to occur, we become less available for the child himself. If teachers are distracted from their jobs by constant vigilance for seizures, they will do their jobs less well for all the children in their charge. This vigilance can be used as a justification for excluding this little boy from a regular classroom—it detracts from the experience of the other children. His desire to be included becomes directly opposed to their need to learn, and remission, oddly, makes this conflict all the more acute. The longer the remission, the more he and his parents can justifiably ask that he be present; on the other hand, the longer the remission, the more anxious teachers and administrators can become about what *may* happen. Infrequent events are always more anxiety-provoking than those with which we deal on a routine basis.

Yet this tension, this worry, is not a direct product of either the remission or the child. It is our own reaction to the remission that creates this state of uncertain anxiety. We wait for something to happen, and don't know when it will come. There are, of course, practical ways we can deal with this anxiety. Firefighters practice over and over again for events that are mercifully rare. Physicians and nurses constantly train themselves and review medical procedures for acute, life-threatening emergencies so that they can act on these with a degree of familiarity and ease. Airports and emergency workers train over and over again for events they profoundly wish will not happen, so that if they do occur they will be ready. In a similar way, the staff of our department can come into Jeffrey's school and prepare the staff so that they could feel more comfortable in the event of some neurological emergency.

Training will deal with only part of the anxiety, however. Jeffrey's visible remission is also a constant reminder of our own *invisible* remissions, of our children's invisible remissions. We are all, in the end, under the same sentence. Sooner or later, quickly or slowly, with or without warning, we will all become ill and die. As Chokyi Nyima Rinpoche, one of the great Tibetan Buddhist teachers in the West, has said, "You cannot find one exception to this. It is true, verifiable. Scientific, if you like. We will all die." All of our children—on whom we pin so much of our hopes, our dreams, our desires, our love, our compassion—all of our children will also become ill and die. As parents, we pray that this is a day we will never see. Children like Jeffrey make us anxious because they remind us that childhood is not a special or privileged era, that children can become ill, can have chronic health problems that threaten them. Children like Jeffrey remind us of our own children's mortality, and we would all prefer not to think about that.

Remission, then, is a teacher if we choose to listen. It can teach the community as a whole, and all of us as individuals, that our time is short. It can teach us that we dare not waste that time in pursuits that distract us from one another. It can teach us where our real treasure lies. Because Jeffrey survived the newborn period, he may be thought of as in a period of remission. And Jeffrey's remission taught his father that his path, seemingly so straightforward, toward ever-more glittering prizes, was in fact a path that led to the wilderness of the soul. Jeffrey's remission taught his father to be more attentive, more open to possibilities, more compassionate. It would be harsh and horrible to say that this spiritual growth in his father justifies the life and suffering Jeffrey experiences; I cannot accept such reasoning. However, to exclude Jeffrey from the community means that we ignore and reject the hard-won lessons his family has learned and how they can now teach us. Remission is the opportunity to listen and see.

Jesus uses his mighty acts of power to convey this message to the community: Whatever you spend your time doing, remember this. This life is short and must be spent well. The illnesses and the infirmities which his mighty acts cure actually just lead to a remission. The paralytic, the woman with the hemorrhage, the daughter of the Syrophoenician woman, the epileptic boy, all are returned to health only to be under the same sentence of death as all the rest of us. Their return to the community imparts a message about the transient nature of all life and all health, and therefore about how we need to spend our precious time.

I grew up with a wonderful blessing that my mother loved to offer: "Time is short and we do not have too much time to gladden the hearts of those who travel the way with us. Be swift to love, and make haste to be kind."

We are all in remission.

Reconciliation. Bringing together that which has been separated is an aspect of healing. This can be between two people: siblings may have quarreled, and later come together, as a result of a parent's illness. We can take the new life that illness produces, the changes in our abilities and capacities, and learn new ways of living our lives. We can draw closer to God, who has always desired us to be close.

My patient Jeffrey has known reconciliation and has helped bring about reconciliation. Jeffrey's father had high hopes and dreams for life with a son. There was a whole range of activities that he had known and enjoyed with his own father, and during his wife's pregnancy he dreamed of passing these on. Time on the water together, fishing. Time walking through the fields together in the fall, hunting. Sports, both watching and playing. The grace of a well-executed double play in baseball, and the elegance of a football pass that evades all defenders and arcs into the hands of the receiver, as if the ball were always meant to be there and nowhere else. Books he had enjoyed, and places he had loved. All of these he dreamed of sharing.

Jeffrey's prematurity made all these dreams feel hollow for a time. Early on, time was spent in a struggle for survival. After that, the acuity of Jeffrey's medical needs kept everyone focused on the tiniest of medical clues and symptoms. But, as time passed and a whole, new life began to reveal itself, Jeffrey's father returned to those dreams. Some seemed simply impossible. Conventional sports were not in the picture for Jeffrey, at least as a participant. Hunting seemed years off for a boy who still spent much of his time in a wheelchair. (Jeffrey's mother had less trouble reconciling herself to this "loss" than did his father.) Fishing, however, seemed within reach. "After all, fishing is in large parts sitting. And he sat well."

Jeffrey's father found that certain challenges could be surmounted. Adaptive equipment could be further adapted to fit the needs of this activity. Lifts and winches, braces and arm rests, clamps and ramps, all could be added to make the family's boat work for the little boy. "Sort of Rube Goldberg meets Jacques Cousteau," said the father.

It would be easy in this process to become so enamored of the modifications, the busyness of the effort, that the time it supported, time together in an activity they both loved, could be lost. Jeffrey's family managed to maintain their focus. The purpose of all these accommodations was to support the family in something that fostered their life together, that reconciled their son's condition to something they wanted to do. These adaptations were not solely for Jeffrey's benefit. The whole family gained from this experience. In the midst of what might have been loss, they found abundance.

In the same way, any time we modify our community's space—physical, mental, or spiritual—to include someone who hasn't been included, we engage in this healing work of reconciliation. We are reconciled to one another when all our community is together.

Acceptance. We often think of acceptance as an internal matter. A family comes to accept its child's limitations; acceptance is viewed as the opposite of denial. Understanding who a child is, what he or she might reasonably be expected to do, what represents a stretch for the child and what represents untenable frustration, is an important part of the life of a family with a child with a serious neurological disorder. However, we often say that a child or a family has unreasonable expectations, when in fact we are the ones in denial. The failure to integrate a child into the community is often our failure of will, imagination, scope. It often represents our own failure to extend ourselves, to be willing to change our ways at little sacrifice save the change itself. Central to our belief is that each of us is infinitely precious in the sight of God. The inclusion of the entire human family in the community is the dream of God. Therefore, we should never say that someone cannot be included in some part of the community, some activity of the community, some function of the community, for anything other than very compelling reasons. To paraphrase G. K. Chesterton, such inclusive practices are not tried and found wanting, merely tried and found difficult.

The inclusion of someone like Jeffrey into a regular classroom requires a few changes: Physical access to the building must be able to accommodate him. Sufficient first-responder training for school personnel must be assured so that his safety is not in question. The school day, the curriculum, and the organization of the day must be evaluated, and changes may be needed. All these changes have a cost. We are very good as communities at determining costs.

We are usually not quite as good at seeing the returns. Physical access, once changed, may allow others to be included as well, now or in the future. Since we never know what our day will entail, the first-responder training may be used in situations unforeseen and unanticipated, that benefit others. The thing about emergencies is that they crop up at unexpected times; more members of the community being prepared may prove useful. Re-examining the curriculum may lead us to see where it has failed others, and lead us to make changes that have far greater impact.

Most important, though, we need to consider the cost of exclusion, of non-invitation. What does it mean about us if we decide that someone is not welcome because of their physical condition, their mental abilities, or any other characteristic? Is this the kind of community we want to be? All of us at some point were helpless, and all of us at some point will be helpless again. In between those moments in the trajectory of our own lives, the failure to accept other people because of their helplessness or vulnerability means we have a peculiar sort of amnesia about our own condition. We fail to look into our own lives, and the lives of those who love us, with clarity when we fail to accept someone with limitations as a member of the community.

Neurological disorders are biological facts, but disabilities are defined by society. Nora Groce provides us an illuminating example of this in her wonderful book *Everyone Here Spoke Sign Language.* In it, she recounts the early history of the community at Chilmark, on Martha's Vineyard. Originally settled by people from Kent, England, the community was afflicted with a particular form of hereditary deafness. Since this form of deafness is a so-called autosomal recessive disorder, it afflicted one fourth of the small community. This form of deafness is associated with no other difficulties; all persons with it are otherwise healthy, of normal intellect, and strong. Because the community's gene pool was small, the trait persisted over the generations with the same frequency.

A community cannot exclude one fourth of its members in a harsh and remote environment; the community would not survive. Therefore, deafness was accepted as a normal part of life. Everyone spoke sign language, so everyone could communicate. Persons with hearing also spoke English, but signing could always be used. Deaf persons were no less deaf; they were simply not functionally disabled because of this fact. Deaf persons held jobs and positions throughout the entire society; they fished, served as town moderator, farmed, and raised children. This society accepted deafness and evolved in a way to adapt to it.

As time passed, however, people from elsewhere arrived in

Chilmark. They brought with them a different set of genes. As time passed, and marriage between original residents and new arrivals became increasingly common, the frequency of deafness began to decrease. Eventually, it reached a point where it was not common enough for the whole society to adapt to it. When that tipping point was reached, when few enough deaf people existed so that those with hearing could imagine a community without them, deafness evolved from biological fact into disability. The deaf were no longer included in all aspects of life.

The point is that we can choose to include or exclude, to accept or reject. Who we choose to accept or reject will say much about us. We can consider where to draw that line in any of a number of ways. We may calculate the financial cost, the degree of intrusion on practices and customs we enjoy; we may pass laws that regulate this behavior.

Jesus offers us another standard: We are to love God with all our heart, all our mind, all our soul, all our strength. That same God has made it abundantly clear that all of humanity is included in God's dream. No one is excluded. Not one. And in case we somehow missed this point, we are told that we are to love our neighbor as ourselves. It would be incomprehensible, foolish beyond all telling, to think that we would not wish to be included as part of the community. So this is the standard, this is the directive. All are to be included—by whatever means at our disposal, with whatever tools we have, with whatever joy and love we can muster, with all the courage we can bring to bear. We are to give all that we are, all that we have, all we can imagine, to bring this to pass.

I spoke with Jeffrey's family after their meeting with the school administrators. It had been difficult, going on for hours. Knowing them a little, I am certain that calmly, quietly, but quite firmly they insisted that Jeffrey be included. In the end, probably exasperated as much as anything else, the school agreed to "give it a try," saying that they would meet again after nine weeks to see if "it was working."

Jeffrey's father said he had smiled, and said, "It already has." The principal was apparently puzzled. "You've thought about my son in a way you wouldn't have, unless we'd pressed this point. He has already become a part of this community, just by this conversation. He is here now."

We are not far away from the kingdom of God.

HE IS GOING AHEAD OF YOU
TO GALILEE

Showing up for Your Life

—ۿۿ—

> As they entered the tomb, they saw a young man,
> dressed in a white robe, sitting on the right side; and
> they were alarmed. But he said to them, "Do not be
> alarmed; you are looking for Jesus of Nazareth, who
> was crucified. He has been raised; he is not here. Look,
> there is the place they laid him. But go, tell his disciples
> and Peter that he is going ahead of you to Galilee; there
> you will see him, just as he told you." So they went out
> and fled from the tomb, for terror and amazement had
> seized them; and they said nothing to anyone, for they
> were afraid.
>
> Mark 16:5–8

One of the best sermons I ever heard was also one of the
shortest. (That is not why it was one of the best.) It was delivered by a hard-bitten old Jesuit, at a school for boys in inner-
city Boston. This man had lived a long and full life as a Jesuit
educator around the globe; he was near the end of his career
at this school for boys from poor neighborhoods. I am certain
that I have met a saint, having met him. It was morning meeting at the school; I was there to do some educational testing of
several students. I had arrived early, and so went to morning
meeting. After prayers had been offered, he stood up, walked
to the podium, and looked around the room. He made eye

contact with a handful of the boys—sometimes a smile, sometimes a quizzical look, sometimes a look of great compassion, sometimes a clear admonition. All of these expressions fluttered across his face quickly—evanescent, like clouds over the sky. The room grew quiet.

"Some people ask me if I think there's a heaven after this life. Harps? Wings? I'm not so sure. It seems kinda doubtful.

"But I do know this. What we do in this life matters. Show up for your life."

Mark's version of the last two weeks of Jesus' life is stark and somewhat harsh. We are led through much of the familiar territory of the other gospels which we tend to hear more often: the triumphant entry into Jerusalem, the casting out of the moneylenders from the temple, the parables that foretell coming events. The departure from Jerusalem and the return. The last supper, the garden of Gethsemane, the arrest, the examination, the trial, the crucifixion. All of this familiar narrative is told in Mark's stark, staccato language, unadorned and straightforward.

The place at which Mark—at least the oldest version of Mark—differs from the other gospels is in the events after the crucifixion. In the oldest version of Mark, there are no appearances after the crucifixion, no resurrection narratives. Later authors, we are told, added these on. Two alternative endings to the gospel, in fact, were added over the years. But the writing, the word choice, the voice give them away as later additions. The original narrative ends as we show above, with the women fleeing in terror. Since we know the story of the Resurrection today, we can assume that at some point they recovered from their fear and told someone what they had seen and heard. Who, how, when, and why are beyond our ability to know.

This much is clear: in Mark's gospel, which we are told clearly at the outset is the *beginning* of the Good News of Jesus Christ, the story ends with an empty tomb, a strange messenger, and a reminder. He is not here, he has been raised. You may see for yourselves. And remember, just as he said, he has gone ahead of you, back to Galilee.

Jesus' three-year period of extraordinary teaching and preaching, his mighty acts of power, his death reserved for political threats to Roman imperial power, his empty tomb—all of these events have led to one place, Galilee, where they all began. The story of Jesus is not one that begins at the margins and leads inexorably to the center, to Jerusalem. Yes, Jesus does enter Jerusalem, first in triumph, later on the way to execution. However, Jerusalem is not the ultimate destination of Jesus' journey; Jerusalem is not the beginning of the Good News that Mark promises us.

Galilee, where the story began, turns out to be the goal. The kingdom of God will not be the Temple restored to holiness, the Romans driven out of Palestine, the reinstitution of the monarchy of King David. The Temple will be restored, and the Romans rendered inconsequential, and the lineage of David reclaimed, but not in the way Jesus' disciples suspected. All of these events will be accomplished by returning to Galilee.

The kingdom of God established by Jesus consisted of communities of faith restored among the poor and the outcast by their own actions, by the transformed lives they led. A community's life was reclaimed by the way they treated one another. The kingdom of God was indeed very near; the generation did not pass but that they tasted of it. Time and again Jesus instructed them, through parables and deeds of power, what this kingdom would be like. And, slowly and hesitantly at first, then with greater conviction and authority, they began to live out this kingdom.

Widows were cared for, orphans raised, the hungry fed, the ill comforted and healed. All this was done by these communities through the power of their transformed hearts. The movement was sufficiently frightening that the Big Tradition in Jerusalem felt its authority threatened. This movement was sufficiently empowering that its leader was pursued and executed by the Roman authorities in a way reserved for those rebels of whom an example was made. The rising of Galilee must have been frightening indeed.

Yet if this movement had been merely a political one, it is doubtful that anyone other than scholars of obscure parts of the Roman Empire would know of it today. Although the message is a radical one—solidarity at a profound level of all humans—it would merely have taken its place along with all the other egalitarian dreams of the oppressed masses throughout human history. The message resonated for its original followers, and it continues to resonate today, because it was delivered by Emmanu-el, God with Us.

The person who led this movement—the enigmatic, itinerant rabbi named Jesus— was at the same time both a historic figure in and of a certain time and the Incarnation of the creator of the universe, the source of love and light and being, who was outside of time and history. His message was so transformative for those who heard it for this reason: the sovereign of the universe was so deeply in love with humanity, with this world, that when all else had failed to redeem it, to return it to the path of love that was the dream of God, that God became incarnate and walked among humans.

The transformative moment for all these followers came when they had an encounter with this Incarnation. When their own incarnation, imperfect as it was, was viewed as so lovely, so important, so profoundly valuable, that God would take incarnate form to rescue them. To restore them. To make them whole and included again.

God becomes incarnate and chooses to inhabit a poor, oppressed, struggling part of the most remote province of the greatest empire of the time. And God spends that Incarnation recklessly, wandering from small town to small town, healing lepers, raising dead children, returning the troubled to their right minds. The only payment requested is this: go, and do likewise. If the Law is summarized as "Love God with all your heart and mind and soul and strength, and love your neighbor as yourself," and the person standing in front of you is both God and your neighbor, the two commandments collapse on top of each other in a dizzying fusion. The power of that fusion led people to go forth and see everyone they encountered as deeply lovely, profoundly valuable, precious in their sight, because they were now seeing with the same eyes, hearing with the same ears, embracing with the same heart, as God. Dissolving into the mind of God, being immersed in the heart of God, changed their lives. They glimpsed the kingdom of God because they incarnated it.

So what then are we to do, we who follow in this same path? How does this message relate to us? We think of the spiritual journey of our lives as leading us far afield. Perhaps we imagine we are to drop everything and go off to Africa, to help care for HIV/AIDS orphans. Or perhaps we think that we should plunge into the inner city, teach school or do some other useful work to redeem the promises made on our behalf about what this poor battered Republic was to look like. We think that following God means going some place far away and removed from the life we have known.

Sometimes it can, but for most of us, I think, this is not the case. I think it is like this: The kingdom of God is very near to us. Wherever we find ourselves, at whatever point in our lives we are, we are close to it. If we cease to be distracted by things which have no more durability than the grass, and focus instead on what is essential, we can see it. If we recognize that everyone we encounter today, and everyone we have ever encountered, and everyone we will ever encounter, is infinitely precious in the sight of God, infinitely valued in the heart of God, infinitely delightful in the mind of God, then we will glimpse the kingdom.

We need to return to our own Galilees. We all encounter the outcast, the poor, the downtrodden, and the lost in our daily lives, the lives we have lived so far. We need to return to those places and encounter Jesus there. He is waiting for us, waiting to join us in the kingdom.

If we remember that every face we see looks at us with the eyes of God, and if we can look at every face we see with the eyes of God, then we will glimpse the kingdom. If we treat everyone with the infinite compassion and lovingkindness with which we are treated, then we will glimpse the kingdom.

The children I have the privilege to see in my medical practice can be viewed as afflicted by a number of disorders, and my job at one level is to identify these disorders. I do this as best I can, as quickly and efficiently as I can, so that we may make better all that can be improved. My job is to be clear—for them, and their parents.

As time has passed, however, I have come to see that such clarity needs to extend beyond the mere facts of the disorders which these children have. I need to be clear about other things.

I need to be clear about who these children are. Their present incarnation is a precious one, no matter what form it takes. No matter how it has been shaped by illness, disease, or disorder, it is precious. Each of these children that I see is a unique manifestation of the dream of God, and must be treated with the dignity and honor that such a guest in my office deserves.

Such a guest needs to be welcomed, embraced, made to feel at home. For the small time we spend together, and everywhere else they travel. No incarnation of the dream of God should ever be excluded from any community, for any community would then be diminished by such an absence. We spend much time in our religious observances inviting God to be with us. God chooses to be with me in the face, in the voice, in the body of everyone I meet. My days are well spent when I remember this; my community is blessed when we all live into this.

I need to be clear about where my patients are. When every person we encounter is made to be welcome, is known to be lovely, is cared for and cherished, then we are present in the kingdom of God. It is not Jerusalem we seek, nor the halls of power, nor some imagined past that never really was. Our own lives, our own communities, our own places are the kingdom of God if we see in this way, act in this way, live in this way. We need to return to our own Galilees, and find Jesus there in the lives of everyone we meet.

Some of the children I have had the privilege to care for still live; some have died. The children and the families in these stories have all given me a glimpse of the kingdom of God, and I pray that they also caught a glimpse of that kingdom through me.

This is the beginning of the Good News: When we care for one another in such a deep and profound way that we can see only the face of the living God in everyone we encounter, and when we treat everyone we meet with the same reverence as we would treat the living God among us, then we have reached the kingdom of God. All else is commentary.

REFLECTION QUESTIONS

If you are using this book as part of a study group, the following questions may help as places to start a conversation. You might also find them provocative for your own reflection.

Introduction

What are your earliest memories of someone with a significant developmental disorder? What were the actions and attitudes of your family regarding such persons? If you were raised in a community of faith, what attitudes did your church teach you—implicitly or explicitly—to take toward such persons?

Certain words that began as precise medical terms, such as *cretin*, *idiot*, or *spastic*, have entered into general usage as insults. Do you ever use, or have you ever used, such words? How do you respond when you hear someone else use such terms to refer to a person? How do you imagine the parent of a child with one of these conditions would feel if they overheard you use the term in casual conversation?

How much does the educational program of your community of faith, for adults or children, rest upon one way of knowing or learning? Is it driven by the assumptions of literacy? For example, could a dyslexic child participate readily in your community's middle-school classes? Could a hyperactive child tolerate your community's second-grade class? Is your adult-education program based on reading or listening to lectures as the primary means of gathering new information?

Miracles

What is your reaction to stories of miraculous healing? Is it different when contemplating stories in Scripture when compared to stories from more recent history or current events, and if so, how or why? Do you believe that the stories recounted in Scripture regarding these "mighty deeds of power" are true? Are they factual? How do you understand them?

Is it easier for you to think about God when you look at something very large, such as the night sky? Is it difficult for you to think about God in the events of your day—your waking, your sleeping, your breathing and eating, your work?

Does the existence of significant disabling disease make you question God's authority in the universe? How do you square a God described as both loving and just with a God who apparently allows infants to suffer and die through such things as hereditary metabolic disease?

Reflect on whether you separate parts of your thinking when it comes to issues of medical care: Do you value the science of medicine and ignore prayer when conditions are treatable—and then turn to prayer and away from science when conditions are serious and without clear medical treatment?

Compassion as a Subversive Activity

Recall a time when you were faced with an injustice, either in your life or the life of someone whom you love. How did you react? How did this injustice make you question your faith in a loving God?

When have you been faced with something bad happening to someone you love, particularly someone who was vulnerable for some reason? How did this crisis make you question your faith in a loving God?

Do you find that you think of social justice and the justice of which Scripture speaks as separate things? Do you connect the stories you hear in your life and on the news with the stories you hear in Scripture? How do you make these connections, if you do? How do you deal with this disconnection, if you don't?

Has your faith in God ever caused you to make a choice that put you at odds with some form of authority, either at work or in your community? How did this happen? What support did you experience from your community of faith, or how did you feel disconnected from the community? How did you make your decision, and what did you do?

Healing as a Political Act

What has been your experience with outcast people? How did you encounter those you have met? How did you respond to them emotionally, intellectually, spiritually, and politically?

Think of someone near to you who developed a serious illness due to some habit over which he or she was unable to take control—such as alcohol, drugs, unhealthy eating or over-eating, workaholism, or cigarettes. What was your reaction to the person and the illness? How did you pray about this?

Have you ever struggled with an addiction? What sort of community were you a part of at that time? How did other people in your community react? How did you experience the reactions of people outside your community?

Think of a time when you were part of a group that excluded someone because of what or who they were, or what they did. How did this decision feel to you then? How do you feel about it now? How did you integrate this action with your faith?

How do you respond to loneliness and isolation in other people? Can you sit with it, or do you feel compelled to try to fix it? Why would God allow people to be lonely?

The Man with the Unclean Spirit

How do you deal with angry people? What do you find yourself feeling when someone is angry with you? How do you react? How do you feel about your own anger?

If your day is a busy one, what do you do to clear your mind and heart when going from one encounter to another? What kinds of feelings do you find you carry from one event to another, and which ones do you usually manage to let go?

What do you do and feel when you are in a supermarket or other public place and you see an adult yelling at a child? A patron yelling at a clerk?

What do you do and feel when you see a group of schoolchildren taunting another child? Would your feelings be different if the child were blind? deaf? in a wheelchair? mentally retarded?

Where is God in the midst of anger?

Simon's Mother-in-law

Bring to mind someone in your life whom you have watched lose the ability to function independently. If you knew the person as active and independent, how did you feel about watching him or her become less able to care for others (perhaps even including you)? Less able to care for himself or herself?

It has been said that our earliest knowledge of God comes from the care we receive as infants. If you have watched a parent or caregiver become frail, how did this make you think about God?

If you have experienced a long period of illness or recuperation, what did feeling well enough to walk again mean for you?

The Leper

Do you know anyone living with HIV/AIDS? When you first heard of the diagnosis, what was your reaction? What were you willing to do to make treatment available for this person?

If your child or spouse, your brother or sister, were diagnosed with HIV/AIDS, what would you do? What would you be willing to do to make treatment available for a loved one?

In our Baptismal vows, we promise to care for the person baptized in some very profound ways. We also promise to resist those forces which corrupt and destroy the creatures of God; the human immunodeficiency virus (HIV) is surely one of those forces. Since our participation in Baptism serves as an outward and visible sign of the way we vow to deal with all of creation, what are you willing to do to make such treatment available for everyone with HIV/AIDS?

The Paralytic

This story concerns a paralyzed young man who cannot be brought to Jesus because the crowd will not make way. As you search your heart, whom have you excluded from the presence of Jesus—by your action or your inaction, your prejudices or your sense of your own preferential entitlement?

The man's friends will not allow him to be excluded, and break through the roof of the house to lower him down. If it were your house, what would you say or do?

When Jesus looked up at the hole in the roof, what expression do you imagine was on his face?

The Man with the Withered Hand

Why do you go to church on Sunday, if you do go? Being as honest as you can, reflect on whether you go seeking solace only, or strength also, pardon only, or renewal also?

If you don't go to church on Sunday, what do you do instead? What does Communion mean to you? What is the Communion of Saints for you—the saints you know in your life?

What is a Sabbath for you?

How is your work a form of prayer? How do you pray when you work?

The Gerasene Demoniac

Call to mind a time when you felt that you wanted to do something new or different, but found that the best contribution you could make was to do what you had always been doing. How did that realization make you feel?

When you think about the people you love, can you picture a common activity they do, an expression they wear, or a gesture they make that always brings a smile to your face and joy to your heart? Imagine God responding that way about you in your daily work and activities.

Think of a way in which you can find meaning and wonder in something you have to do every day. How might you pay attention to this activity today?

The Woman with the Hemorrhage and Jairus' Daughter

Whom have you helped without being aware of it at the time? When you think back on this experience, what were you doing and feeling at the time? How did you become aware that you had provided some kind of assistance? How did knowing this change your understanding of community?

When you offer the peace at Communion, how do you choose to greet people? What do you say? What do you want your hands and arms to say?

Have you ever avoided touching someone because of his or her appearance? Why? If every part of creation is beautiful in God's sight, how do you understand your own reaction?

The Ill of Gennesaret

When have you experienced a community that was not your own? What was the experience like? What customs and habits were interesting? Attractive? Confusing? Disturbing? How did you understand this experience in light of our Baptismal vows, which do not make much of such differences?

If your child were hurt or injured, what would you do for him or her? Since our Baptismal vows underline our common family, how do you understand your responsibility for other people's children?

Children make up a quarter of the population of the United States, but research into children's diseases is supported by only 12 percent of the funds available. How do you evaluate these statistics in the context of your Baptismal vows?

The Syrophoenician Woman's Daughter

We often talk of the "deserving poor." What does this phrase mean to you? Can someone be undeserving of our help? How would you decide who was undeserving?

When groups of people insist on taking their place in our society, we often feel anxious or angry. We say that we have achieved something, and they should try to do the same. One of our prevailing national myths is that we all start life equally and fairly. What is unearned privilege? Does it ever work to your advantage?

Thomas Jefferson said, "When I consider that God is just, I tremble for my country." What do you think he meant by this?

Can a person do something that excludes him or her from the love of God? If so, what might that be?

The Deaf-Mute

Whom have you failed to see as a member of the community? How did that exclusion come about? Was it a result of the way you were taught as a child? Of your experiences as a young person? Of your desire to preserve some privilege you have earned?

Is there any individual or group that you have felt free to exclude from your heart? your prayers? Why?

If you have ever been excluded, what reason did a group use to exclude you? How did you respond to being excluded? What effects does this experience of exclusion continue to have in your life today? In your view, where was God in that experience?

The Blind Man

Whom have you failed to really see when you first looked at him or her? As you think of how you came to see a situation more clearly, why had you misperceived it in the first place? Sometimes we see only what we expect to see. What expectations do you have in your daily life that lead you to misperceive the world around you?

Can you describe the face and the eyes of the last person who asked you for money on the street? The last person who filled your order in a restaurant?

The Epileptic Boy

What particular situations most challenge your belief in a loving God? When does unbelief come to sit on your shoulder and whisper in your ear? In what part of your life do you feel furthest from God?

When do you feel helpless—in what part of your life is this feeling most vivid? How can you pray at a time like that?

Having to watch your child suffer from a serious illness is something all parents fear. If you are a parent, how does this fear manifest itself? Do you ever pray about this fear? Is it part of your life hidden in God?

Blind Bartimaeus

Recall a time when you were caught short in your assumptions about someone. When you look back on this experience, what led you to your incorrect assumptions? What was it about the person, the situation, and yourself that made you underestimate someone? How did you respond when you realized what you had done?

In your daily life, with what individuals do you most often interact? What do you know about them, and their inner life? After your initial acquaintance, did you stop learning new things about them? Did you stop telling new things about yourself?

The people you see today may be all you see of God today. How will you spend that time? Make an intention.

What does it mean to be faithful? How are you faithful in your life? In which aspects of your life is faithfulness a struggle?

You Are Not Far from the Kingdom of God

Describe an experience when everything you had planned fell apart. How did you react? How did you try to come to terms with the situation?

Where do you find meaning in your life, from day to day? Are these interests and activities the sorts of things you can count on? What if they were lost, or became impossible for you to continue? What would you do? How would you think about your life afterward?

We spend much of our lives trying to accumulate things we will eventually have to leave behind. What do you acquire? Why? When your children or partner or friends think of you, what image do you think comes to their minds?

If you have children, what do you pray for in their lives? If you have parents still living, what do you pray for in their lives?

If earning a living became unnecessary for you tomorrow, what would still be present in your life? Would your life continue to be fulfilling?

How do you punctuate your day so you stay awake?

He Is Going Ahead of You to Galilee

Where and when do you "show up" for your life? When have you failed to "show up" for your life?

What do you make sure you do every day? Do you eat a meal with your family? Do you exercise? Do you make sure that the last word your family or partner hears from you as you part company is an expression of love? Do you pray? What else?

One of the great eastern European rabbis asked his students how they knew when the dawn was breaking. "When you can tell a sheep from a goat," said one. No, the rabbi said, not then. "When you can tell an oak from a pine tree," said another. No, said the rabbi, not then either. A young student, usually quiet and thought of as slow by his fellows, said, "Rabbi, I think it is when you look into the face of another and can see nothing but a brother or a sister." The rabbi smiled. When you next see someone, will the dawn break for you?